BEYOND CAPE HORN

THE ATLANTIC
ADVENTURES
OF

LE DAUPHIN AMICAL

DON DOUGLASS

WITH

MARGIE MANZONI
&
RÉANNE HEMINGWAY-DOUGLASS

Published by Cave Art Press, Anacortes, WA 98221
An imprint of Douglass, Hemingway & Co., LLC
CaveArtPress.com

ISBN 978-1934199-190

Scribe, editor, and book designer: Lisa Wright
Transcription ace and additional contributor: Arlene Cook
Manuscript reader: Kathleen Kaska
Cover photo by William Van Ryssen
Drawings by Margy Gates

Table of Contents

You can't take a sunshot sitting in the shade!

-DCD

Introduction

Beyond Cape Horn: the Atlantic Voyages of Le Dauphin Amical recounts the 1975-1976 voyages of the ketch *Le Dauphin Amical* (*The Friendly Dolphin*) east and west across the Atlantic Ocean. We sailed from the Patagonian port city of Punta Arenas, Chile, to Cape Town, South Africa, and back through the Panama Canal to Long Beach, California, with numerous stops and adventures along the way.

When my wife Réanne Hemingway-Douglass and I first set out in *Dolphin* from Los Angeles, we intended to sail around the world via the Southern Hemisphere. After getting flipped end-over-end in a pitchpole accident 800 miles off the coast of southern Chile, our crippled boat limped into Punta Arenas for temporary repairs. Réanne wrote an account of the voyage, *Cape Horn—One Man's Dream, One Woman's Nightmare,* in 1994. It was reissued in a second, updated edition in 2004 and has become a classic of nautical true-adventure literature.

Beyond Cape Horn is a sequel to Réanne's book. It tells the story of the rest of *Dolphin*'s trip, from South America to Africa, and home to California. This story is based on the recollections of three people: me, Don Douglass, *Dolphin*'s skipper; Réanne Hemingway-Douglass, my wife then and now, and my first mate as far as Buenos Aires; and Margaret (Margie) Manzoni. South African-born, Margie signed on in Punta Arenas and sailed with me for the rest of *Dolphin*'s voyage. Forty years on, we each have different recollections of our adventures, reflecting our subjective experiences. Untrustworthy memories have been supplemented with paper records, especially the daily ship's log that I kept throughout the voyage, as well as with extracts from our diaries.

Though this book describes a voyage that was less of an ordeal than Réanne's story—and the weather was better—Margie, Réanne and I hope that it might achieve comparable success, and be read with at least as much enjoyment.

-                                 DCD, Anacortes, 2015

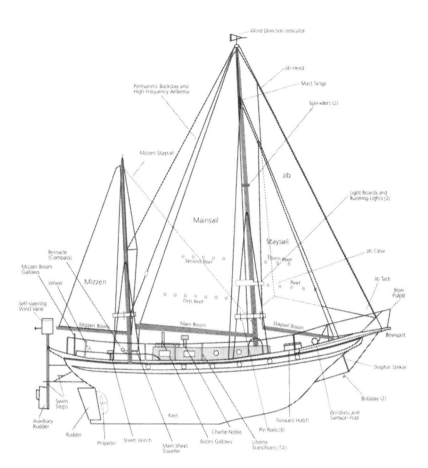

Le Dauphin Amical (Dolphin) exterior layout

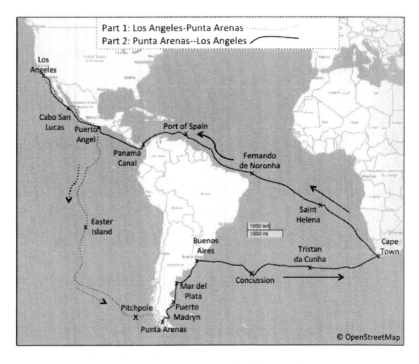

Voyages of *Le Dauphin Amical* 1974-1976

Prologue

Winter had already begun in the Southern Hemisphere as my wife, Réanne, and I sailed northeast through the Strait of Magellan on our forty-two foot ketch, *Le Dauphin Amical (the Friendly Dolphin)*. Five days of sailing from Punta Arenas, Chile, would lead us out into the open Atlantic. Réanne and I had already spent six months on the voyage that was my life's ambition—a circumnavigation of the Southern Hemisphere. We'd sailed south from Los Angeles in October of 1974, along the coast of Mexico, and spent a month at Easter Island. We then sailed southeast across the Southern Ocean, intending to round Cape Horn and head across the South Atlantic to Cape Town, South Africa. Instead, *Dolphin* pitchpoled (flipped completely upside-down) in a violent storm 800 miles west of Cape Horn. After a five week struggle through the archipelagos of southern Chile, Réanne and I reached the small port city of Punta Arenas in our disabled boat, Unfortunately, *Dolphin* was too severely damaged to be overhauled at the limited facilities available there. We spent two months carrying out temporary repairs, hired three additional crewmembers, and headed for a better equipped boatyard in Buenos Aires, Argentina, a thousand miles to the north. This book is the story of *Dolphin*'s continuing voyage, from South America to Africa and back to California via the Panama Canal.

There are certainly easier and cheaper ways to travel around the world than by small sailboat. In spite of this, the delight of messing about in boats and the romance of distant shores has inspired many an adventurer to dream of a circumnavigation, including me.

Another reason I love sailing is my desire to experience life to the fullest, right to the fine edge that divides success from failure. The mental and physical fascination of ocean sailing provide me the challenge I crave. The ocean is the final judge of every sailor's skill. As the California singer-songwriter David Crosby once said, "You can't bullshit the ocean. It's not listening."

My service in the U.S. Army only reinforced my innate rejection of external authority. My earliest sailing experiences taught me that the captain of a small sailboat has more independence and responsibility than most people experience in a lifetime. It's just me and my boat against the unforgiving sea.

*   *   *   *   *

I started sailing as a kid in Los Angeles in the 1940s. My family didn't have a lot of money, but for a while I had a little plywood dinghy, and I spent my free time learning how to handle it. Dinghy sailing is the best way to develop instinctive boat-handling skills because a mistake is instantly punished with a capsize. When I was first learning to sail, I flipped the dinghy repeatedly, but as I developed more competence, I became the master of my little boat and sailed it even in stormy weather. One particularly windy afternoon, I took my dinghy out into Ventura Harbor and capsized in full view of the posh Ventura Yacht Club bar. While I was righting the dinghy, my seat cushions blew away downwind. I left the dinghy to swim after them, and the dinghy promptly capsized again. The cushions blew away again while I was re-righting the dinghy, and again the dinghy capsized when I swam after them. This farce went on for a while, until someone from the yacht club phoned the harbormaster, who arrived in a launch.

"Hey, kid!" he hollered, "Get in my boat. I'm going to tow you back in! It's too windy for you!"

"No way!" I yelled back, "I can do this. Just hang onto my dinghy while I get my cushions." I wouldn't give up, and I finally managed to recapture my cushions while the guy held my dinghy. I sailed triumphantly back to the slip by myself.

*   *   *   *   *

The sailing exploits of my teenage years were a welcome escape from the confining world of school and part-time jobs. I read a great book in high school about two guys who sailed a big ketch from California to the South Seas. They lived the dream of sailing adventure, no teachers, no bosses, and lots of beautiful girls! That sounded like the life I wanted to lead.

However, everyday life somehow got in the way. As a grown man, saddled with work and family responsibilities, I still dreamed of recapturing my carefree youth by sailing around the world. Sailing's ultimate test, a circumnavigation of the Southern Hemisphere via Cape Horn, was the adventure I'd dreamed about my whole life. My family and I could spend a year visiting tropical ports and enjoying endless free time to read and relax during the long ocean crossings. The experience would also challenge us, since blue water sailing is one of the supreme tests of human endurance and ingenuity. We spent eighteen months in preparation, and set off on the trip of a lifetime.

Chapter 1

Le Dauphin Amical

During my first date with Réanne, I asked her what she considered to be the most important thing in life. Without hesitation, Réanne answered, "Love." She returned the question, and my immediate reply was "Adventure." As it turned out, we've had plenty of both in the nearly fifty years we've been together, although at times the adventures have been more than either of us bargained for.

I met Réanne Hemingway in 1966. I was the divorced father of three teenagers, and she was the divorced mother of two boys. Réanne's background and personality could not have been more different from mine—she came from an educated family and had lived a cultured life, playing the piano and living in France. I could tell she had plenty of determination since she was raising her two sons on her own.

At the conclusion of our second date—a rappelling class in the Sierras—I gave Réanne a copy of the book *Once is Enough*, by Miles and Beryl Smeaton. It's a classic true-story maritime adventure about the Smeaton's experiences sailing their yacht, *Tzu Hang*, around the world. They survived two pitchpoles. A pitchpole is an accident in which waves flip the boat end-over-end. Would Réanne consider going on a sailboat adventure around the world with me? "I might," she said, "but not the pitchpoling part." At that time I was an engineer working for an aerospace instrument company and completely broke. Réanne married me several months later under the assumption that the idea of sailing around the world together would be only a dream. She was even more certain about it after I was laid off from my engineering job two years later. Her salary as a high school French and English teacher was the only thing that kept us and our five kids financially afloat for the next couple of years.

Less than a decade later, however, my dream became a reality. After I lost my job, I enrolled at Claremont Graduate School and earned a master's degree in business economics. For my graduate thesis, I combined my love of outdoor adventure with my inherent sense of entrepreneurship and wrote a business plan for a company that would manufacture and retail hiking and camping gear tailored to the Southern California market. I knew I would find working for myself to be much more rewarding than working as a little engineering cog in a huge corporate machine. I also had faith in my ability to develop a successful business. Réanne and I found investors to back us in this enterprise, which we called Wilderness Group, Inc. (WGI), and within two years we were making real money. Managing a growing enterprise was an exciting adventure, but I was still constrained by the daily grind—by my overly scheduled existence and the need to satisfy vendors and investors. I spent as much time as I could on strenuous expeditions, sailing, skiing, hiking and climbing, but that wasn't enough to satisfy my need for physical challenge. From the outset, I had told Réanne and our partners that once annual sales reached a million dollars, I would buy a sailboat, take an extended leave from the company, and set off for Cape Horn and beyond. This became a reality in 1975. I had achieved the necessary success to escape the business world, and by then my goal had expanded to include the whole family in my adventure.

Not long after we married, Réanne and I bought a share in a small sailboat called *Olé*. We took our family on many short cruises in the pleasant waters of Southern California, but I was still determined to fulfill my boyhood ambition of sailing around the world by way of Cape Horn. I knew I'd need a more substantial vessel than *Olé* for the trip, so when our financial situation was right, Réanne and I spent several months scouring the want ads and talking to yacht brokers up and down the West Coast. I settled on a 20-ton, 42-foot (50-foot overall) wooden-hulled ketch called *Liddie Mae*. The boat was only two years old with a design by the renowned British Columbian naval architect, William Garden. Her owner, a retired Navy officer from Seattle, had intended to sail her around the world. However, he realized within a day or two of leaving home that he simply wasn't prepared for such an undertaking. He turned around and headed back to port, and *Liddie Mae* sat in a San Francisco marina until Réanne and I decided to buy her.

She was an ugly boat with dull grey paint and a squat cabin, but she had a hull solidly constructed from lengths of 2-inch wide and $1^{5/8}$-inch thick Port Orford cedar glued and nailed together in a strip-planked design onto stout oak frames. I wanted a vessel that could withstand the rigors of Cape Horn and the Southern Ocean, and I was sure *Liddie Mae* would do better than the newer fiberglass designs that were just starting to enter the market. I also approved of her reliable 36-horsepower Perkins diesel engine—and her price was right. We sailed her south to Newport Beach and set about remodeling her into the sort of vessel I had in mind for our adventure. My over-riding concern was seaworthiness, so I hired an engineer friend, Al Ryan, to help make her even sturdier. Though we didn't have cash to burn, my instructions to Al were to spare no expense when it came to safety. One of Al's suggestions was to add a 3-inch steel upright pole salvaged from a scrapped Navy destroyer between the hull and the cabin roof. This modification helped save our lives later in the voyage.

Liddie Mae was ketch-rigged, meaning that she had a main mast forward and a shorter mizzenmast aft. Many different sail configurations are possible with this type of ketch rig and this flexibility let the boat travel efficiently in a wide variety of wind and sea conditions. The main mast supported both the mainsail and several types of headsails, from our largest headsail, the genoa, through a twin jib combination, to the minimal storm sail, while the mizzen sail added to the maximum sail area of 11,000 square feet. I made sure that we could rig preventers, which are straps that control the boom. They are used when sailing downwind, and keep the boom from being blown across the cockpit in an unintentional gybe, perhaps injuring crew or damaging equipment (See the Glossary at the end of the book for definition of sailing terms, and the diagram at the end of the Introduction that names the various parts).

I also wanted the best possible equipment on our boat, though I was wary of relying on electronic navigation aids that would be impossible to repair or replace if they failed mid-ocean. Similarly, I opted for kerosene lamps rather than corrosion-prone electrical lighting. I placed my reliance on traditional seamanship and proven equipment that I could repair and maintain by myself. I wanted to be able to get replacement parts in any ship's chandlery in any small fishing village in any corner of the world, and not be dependent on having fancy equipment shipped in from Los Angeles at great cost in time and money.

Our four boys also worked on the boat, stripping and sanding off the gray paint and re-painting it a gleaming white. Réanne continued her full-time teaching career, but she also assumed the role of Chief Steward. She was responsible for planning all of the meals and purchasing six months' worth of food supplies for six people. All of the cans had to be painted with several layers of shellac to protect them from seawater.

Réanne also insisted on renaming the boat. No one liked the name *Liddie Mae,* and Réanne wanted something French. She loved the language and she also thought a French name might generate goodwill in all the French-speaking places we hoped to visit. Her suggestion was *Le Dauphin Amical (The Friendly Dolphin),* after William Garden's name for his ketch design: *Porpoise.* As it happened, we didn't visit any French-speaking places during the voyage, and *Le Dauphin Amical* was a difficult name to use over the radio, so we ended up referring to the boat by her English name, *Friendly Dolphin,* or just *Dolphin.*

Preparations for the voyage took us eighteen months. I was willing to invest plenty of time in getting ready, after reading about so many would-be voyagers who set out under-prepared. Réanne continued working as a teacher while I oversaw the boat preparations, ran our WGI business, and continued to train myself mentally and physically for the expedition with a variety of outdoor pursuits (climbing, hiking, and teaching classes in outdoor survival skills). I was so busy that Réanne complained I didn't have any time left for her or our kids. But I convinced Réanne that the trip would bring us all closer together, and that she should be a part of it. As we tied up the loose ends, I began to imagine the adventures that lay ahead. How many families would ever experience a round-the-world sailing voyage? It was the chance of a lifetime!

Le Dauphin Amical at anchor

Chapter 2

Los Angeles, California to Punta Arenas,

Chile

12 October 1974 - 5 April 1975

Our adventure started even before we left Los Angeles. The weekend prior to our departure we took some friends with us on a cruise to Catalina Island. I was thinking about the voyage ahead and concerned that Réanne, the boys, and I had yet to do a real Man Overboard (MOB) drill. All of us knew the procedures: one person pointing at the victim, circling the boat, coming safely alongside, and using appropriate hoisting techniques. We had practiced retrieving a hat a few times, but it seemed like pretending. So, on this last weekend, I told everybody as we left the harbor that we'd have a proper MOB drill. Then I said nothing more about it. Later, when all the sails were up and everybody was relaxed and the adults were drinking wine, I went below, put on a life vest, came up through the forward hatch and quietly slipped overboard. I was lucky that someone happened to look up and see me receding in the wake. It took some time for the crew to turn the boat around and pick me up. In fact, they had to make several passes, and it took *ninety minutes* before I was hauled back on board. It could have been worse. Other friends of ours, a couple from Oregon, had to do a

MOB for real after the husband fell overboard in a full-blown storm. The wife was unable to retrieve him, and he drowned. I was appalled that lack of preparation had cost a man's life.

Our circumnavigation began on October 12, 1974. My goal was the same one I had described to Réanne on the night we met: to sail around the world, via Cape Horn. Our daughter Dawn was in college in Alaska by that time, and our oldest son Chris was in the Army, but our younger boys, Jeff, Mike, and Sean set out with us, along with Sean's friend, Carl.

Like all wooden-hulled boats, *Dolphin* leaked a little around various fittings, as the hull and cabin frame shifted under the stresses of the winds and waves. The crew emptied the bilges as needed using a manual pump that was operated with a wooden handle from a cramped position in a little space under the radio locker. Early in the voyage, the bilges needed only occasional pumping, but as we sailed along the coast of Mexico, *Dolphin* scraped across an uncharted rock. One of the hull planks was damaged, and several joints seemed to have sprung loose. Jeff and I epoxied over the damaged planks, but seawater now leaked in at a rate of about fifty gallons a day, requiring longer and more frequent spells of pumping. Sometimes this meant more than a hundred strokes, or about five minutes, once or twice a day. I routinely recorded the amount of water we pumped in the logbook, just to make sure the leak wasn't getting worse.

Friction between my teen-aged crew and me developed almost as soon as we left Los Angeles. The boys were not enthusiastic about the hard work of blue water sailing. I knew that the severe weather and huge waves in the high latitudes around Cape Horn would make this a grueling expedition, and I tried to drill the crew in quick responses to emergency situations and heavy weather. I hadn't realized that my crew didn't share my desire to test themselves against the extreme conditions *Dolphin* would find. My older son, Jeff, seemed eager to make the voyage. He compared rounding Cape Horn to climbing Mt. Everest—it was something to attempt "because it's there." The other three boys were much more ambivalent, and not interested in following my orders. Ultimately, all four boys, including Jeff, quit the trip within the first six weeks, even before we'd left Mexico. I took their desertion hard. We'd had the foresight to insist that each kid save enough money to fly home if he quit the voyage, and they had already made alternate living arrangements for the time Réanne and I would be away.

After the boys abandoned the project, the voyage with just the two of us went quite well, at least in terms of sailing. The weather was pleasant, and I could set the sails and self-steering gear so that *Dolphin* practically sailed herself. Of course, there was still plenty of physical work, from pumping the bilges to fixing meals, from maintaining all the gear to fine-tuning the sails. This was tough on Réanne. With just the two of us aboard, she had to do more of the physical work, and in spite of the pleasant conditions, she was seasick much of the time. I've never been seasick in my life, and I thought the problem was all in her head. In retrospect, I was awfully tough on her. I also had to acknowledge that the dream of circumnavigating via Cape Horn was mine alone. Réanne was along for the ride because she loved me.

On January 6, thirty-two days and 3,500 miles out of Acapulco, we sighted land—Easter Island! I was proud of my navigation, having gotten us there with just a sextant, Nautical Almanac, Sight Reduction Tables, and time ticks provided by a radio, as our chronometer turned out to be unreliable. (See Appendix 2 for a discussion of Celestial Navigation). Emotionally, the trip had been tougher. After we left Acapulco, Réanne and I argued a lot about continuing to sail around the world with just the two of us. She couldn't make up her mind whether or not to fly home from Easter Island, and I didn't want to be manipulated by Réanne's refusal to commit. I was determined to continue around Cape Horn, even single-handedly if I had to, although I worried that it might be too big a challenge. Just keeping the boat sailing was a full-time, physically demanding job. The never-ending pumping of the bilges and the below-deck chores like cooking required at least one other person aboard at a minimum. I looked for suitable crew during the month we were on Easter Island, but couldn't find anyone with the appropriate skills and personality. Figuring I'd have to go on to Cape Horn alone, I was elated when Réanne decided to come with me after all, at least until her year-long teaching sabbatical was up. She told me she loved me too much to let me risk trying to round the Horn alone. She made the brave decision to follow her heart on a voyage filled with hard work, discomfort, and danger. I had assumed she was going to abandon me, so I'd tried to break the emotional connection between us by being gruff and unkind to her. I joked that if I ever tried a trip like this again, I'd hire an all-girl crew, since they wouldn't argue with me as much as my wife did, and they'd be less likely to leave me and go off on their own.

Dolphin departed Easter Island on February 3, 1975 and set sail for Cape Horn. I plotted a course that I hoped would keep us sailing in moderate weather and seas, but we also had to be prepared for extreme conditions as we reached higher latitudes. The sailing was good for the first week or so. Réanne and I got along better than we had on the first leg of the voyage. I was delighted to have her with me and I tried to let her know that I appreciated her contributions. Repair and maintenance were constant, and I told Réanne that facing this experience alone would have been both frightening and exhausting. I wasn't sure I could have handled it alone.

After two weeks of sailing due south with the wind blowing from the west, we made "the big left turn" southeast toward Cape Horn. Each day I tried to calculate our position, but this was possible only when I could get a "sun shot" at noon with my sextant. Since our chronometer was unreliable, and atmospheric conditions precluded reception of regular time ticks on the shortwave radio, my estimates of our longitudinal position were uncertain. Sailing became more challenging, too, with rain squalls, hail, enormous rolling seas, and gale force winds of 35-40 knots (See Appendix 3 for definition of the Beaufort Wind Speed Scale). Réanne accused me of thriving on the excitement, but as conditions continued to deteriorate and fatigue set in, I found it increasingly difficult to find much fun in what we were doing.

Réanne steering *Dolphin*

On February 26, I figured we were only a week away from Cape Horn. That afternoon we crossed the 50°S parallel, meaning that in terms of latitude, we were further south than New Zealand, Australia and South Africa. We also sailed into the worst storm we had encountered yet. Huge, confused seas tossed *Dolphin* violently, and gusts of seventy knots or more shrieked in the rigging. I went over emergency procedures with Réanne. She was pretty frightened and argued that there wouldn't be much point in using the life raft since we'd die of hypothermia and nobody would know what had happened to us. The latter prospect worried her more than dying itself.

At midnight that night I jotted a short entry in the ship's log: "Seas building and more violent, like Force 9. Tumbling crests and large white patches. Driving rain."

Half an hour later (0030 hours, February 27): "Transom taking pounding. Gusts flattening the boat for several seconds at a time. Terrific screaming noise."

Waves bashed *Dolphin* mercilessly, and the rolling was terrific. I locked the cabin shut from the inside, and Réanne and I wedged ourselves into our berths with no choice but to endure the wild ride.

My log entry for 0200 states baldly: "Boat rolls over being thrown through foam wave crest." In other words, we had done just what the Smeatons had: we had pitchpoled.

Neither Réanne nor I were hurt, and the boat righted itself. The cabin was flooded knee deep, swirling with a chaotic mess of debris. Seawater continued to stream in through the broken portlights, but the hull and keel seemed intact and—incredibly—the two masts were still standing. *Dolphin* must have been thrown completely upside-down, so that the masts pitched almost vertically into the ocean. The steel reinforcement we'd installed during *Dolphin*'s refit had kept the cabin roof from being crushed. Réanne worked the bilge pump steadily while I checked for further damage, and then poured buckets of water from the cabin floor down the sink drain. We ate soggy chocolate bars for energy. After we emptied the cabin, we rested for the next couple of hours, looking forward to the daylight. Réanne's memoir, *Cape Horn—One Man's Dream, One Woman's Nightmare*, describes the incident and our subsequent struggle to reach a safe harbor. My own recent autobiography, *Sailing Off the Anchor*, also describes the event.

The first five days after the accident were a struggle for basic survival, as we sailed due east toward the Chilean mainland under jury rig, uncertain whether the boat would remain afloat, and equally uncertain of our position until we sighted the coast of southern Chile. When we finally spotted land, I used our indispensable guidebook, the *South American Pilot*, to fix our position. This was difficult since the daylight hours were short and the visibility was hampered by ceaseless rain and fog. Using compass bearings and descriptions of landmarks in the pilot book, I determined we had arrived at a large natural channel known as Golfo Trinidad. With some difficulty, we navigated our way through the entrance and found an anchorage, Dársena Aid (Aid Basin), where we stayed for the next week getting our damaged boat as shipshape as we could manage, replenishing our water supplies, and recovering our energies. We debated what to do next. Neither Réanne nor I were in any condition to tackle Cape Horn, nor could we tell how seriously *Dolphin* had been damaged. Valparaiso, Chile, the nearest large city, was a thousand miles north, across open ocean. We could sit in Dársena Aid and wait for help, but for how long? Eventually we agreed that our best option was self-rescue. This meant we had to sail south through the Patagonian equivalent of Alaska's Inside

Passage to the port of Punta Arenas, a small Chilean city on the Strait of Magellan, where I hoped we could undertake boat repairs.

It took us more than three weeks to wend our way south through about 400 miles of Patagonian channels and straits from Dársena Aid to Punta Arenas and civilization. Although it wasn't like being on the open ocean, every single day challenged us with gusty winds and strong currents. I used the logbook to record the number of pump strokes it took to empty the bilges. The bilges filled to their fifty-gallon capacity in about an hour, and they filled even faster when the waves were rough. The constant pumping exhausted Réanne. The pitchpole had probably worsened the existing damage from our encounter with the Mexican rocks. Two cargo ships passed us by without stopping to offer assistance, in spite of the international distress flag flying in *Dolphin*'s rigging. A few days later, a third ship, UK-registered *Bendoran*, stopped alongside us. Réanne clambered up a rope ladder with a plastic bag full of messages we had prepared two weeks earlier to be radioed to family and friends. While Réanne enjoyed tea and scones with *Bendoran*'s master, Captain Addison, and his wife, I worked my butt off loading drums of much-needed diesel fuel, along with six rolls of toilet paper, a kettle of hot soup, and a bottle of Scotch whisky sent along by the Captain. I was anxious about the way *Dolphin* was tied to *Bendoran*, so I cast off as soon as Réanne had climbed back down the long ladder. Neither Réanne nor I were Scotch drinkers, but after enjoying the hearty soup that night, we shared Captain Addison's bottle, happily toasting *Bendoran* and her crew.

The weather rarely let up for the remaining 300 miles, but we felt more relaxed once we knew that our families had heard via the *Bendoran's* radio operator that we were alive and well. I assumed we could get the boat repaired in Punta Arenas. I asked Réanne how she felt about continuing on our original itinerary to the Falklands and South Africa. She hesitated and pointed out that her teaching sabbatical ended in September, only five months away. I suggested she should apply for another year of unpaid leave. Réanne headed off further argument by suggesting we put off any decision-making until we got to Punta Arenas and could get an idea about how long *Dolphin's* repairs would take.

On March 29, we entered the Strait of Magellan. This is an immense and formidable stretch of water that includes the notoriously unstable channel known as Paso Inglés, or English Passage, where the Atlantic Ocean meets the Pacific. We found the Strait ruggedly beautiful, with steep granite walls topped by snowfields and glaciers, but it was a tough place for a small sailboat. After rounding Cabo Froward—the southernmost tip of the South American continent—we veered north, but opposing winds forced us to hole up at anchor for another several days.

On April 4 the weather abated slightly and we ventured back into the Strait, spurred on, at least in part, by the fact that we had once again run out of toilet paper. Punta Arenas was now less than thirty miles away and as we got closer, I worried what would happen when we arrived. *Dolphin* was no longer just a pleasure yacht passing through, but a boat in need of extensive repairs. Would we be able to extend our transit visas? Could we get the repairs we needed? The *South American Pilot* wrote that the only marine facility at Punta Arenas was an open pier extending out into the channel, rather than an enclosed harbor, so *Dolphin* would be exposed to the winds and waves of the Strait of Magellan.

Dolphin tied ahead of a Chilean Navy vessel, Punta Arenas, Chile

We tied up at the pier in front of a Chilean Navy cruiser. The sailors aboard waved at us and cheered. Réanne began to cry as we realized that the dock was crowded with people all there to greet us. A port official handed us a bag of mail. People offered to drive us wherever we wanted to go. Television reporters stuck microphones in our faces and asked questions about our ordeal. Réanne, who spoke Spanish in addition to French, answered them as best she could, but my own answers would have been the same as hers. When someone asked her how she felt, she replied, trying not to cry, that we were very, very happy to be here. Then she pulled me over to her, gave me a hug and added, "*Mi esposo es muy buen marinero!* My husband is a great sailor!" I was both proud and delighted to hear her say this, and my optimism soared.

Chapter 3

Punta Arenas, Chile

4 April - 7 June, 1975

Our arrival in Punta Arenas marked the end of my "Cape Horn" aspirations. Surviving the month-long trial of navigating our crippled boat through remote Patagonia into a safe harbor was adventure enough for the time being. I was positive that after her repairs, *Dolphin* would still be the perfect sturdy and seaworthy vessel required for sailing around the world. I would merely modify the route so that we circumnavigated via the Strait of Magellan, rather than rounding Cape Horn. In my opinion, the pitchpole had been a serious wake-up call, but not a knock-out blow. It was only a matter of getting *Dolphin* properly overhauled and finding more crew, and then we could set off for Cape Town, South Africa, and the next leg of the trip. Réanne was less certain. She had found our great adventure much more of an ordeal than I had. She didn't share my dream of circumnavigation, or my confidence in its feasibility. We continued to argue about the future of the voyage and our future together while we assessed *Dolphin*'s needs.

Our first chores in Punta Arenas were bureaucratic: we had to check in with port authorities, Interpol, and the Chilean Navy, whose guests we would be during our stay. The man who had handed us our mail on our arrival introduced himself as the port captain's assistant and offered to drive us directly to the office of Admiral Allen, the local head of the Chilean Navy. Unfortunately, although Réanne and I were safe, *Dolphin* was not. The pier's position left *Dolphin* exposed to the wind and waves, and I was extremely hesitant to leave her. The barometer had dropped since morning, and a strong north wind was kicking up swells that pounded the hull against the dock. At the suggestion of one of the dockworkers, I heaved an anchor over the starboard stern to keep the boat feathered into the wind. A naval cadet was assigned to watch over the boat in our absence.

I knew our sixty-four day passage from Easter Island to Punta Arenas had been pretty slow, but it cheered me when Admiral Allen told me he thought our hundreds of miles sailing in the Patagonian channels might be a new cruising record. I was also proud that we had reached Punta Arenas under our own power with the only assistance coming from the crew of *Bendoran*. Admiral Allen told us that *Dolphin* was only the fourth sailboat to arrive in Punta Arenas that year, and that the other three boats had all experienced problems too. One yacht had spent fifteen days trying to enter the Strait of Magellan from the Atlantic side and had been blown back three times. Another boat had to be towed the last 200 miles into port. A third yacht, *Whisper*, was several months ahead of *Dolphin* on a planned voyage around South America. Sailed by a California couple, Hal and Margaret Roth, she had dragged anchor and run aground only fifteen miles from Cape Horn. A Chilean naval patrol spotted the Roths and crew after they'd spent nine days living as castaways. *Whisper* was loaded onto a patrol boat and taken to the small Chilean town of Puerto Williams for repairs. I felt even prouder of our achievements when Admiral Allen told me he was going to use our experiences as an example of good seamanship to the naval cadets under his command.

Admiral Allen assigned Commander Corthron of the Chilean Navy rescue tugboat *Colocolo* to be our liaison while we were guests of the Chilean Navy in Punta Arenas. Commander Corthron was a great talker, entertaining and amusing. He spoke British English peppered with Yankee slang expressions picked up from three years of training in Pensacola, Florida, and a year in Philadelphia. Réanne and I grew quite fond of him, and he was immensely helpful in solving some of our logistical problems, including obtaining our replacement chronometer. We had ordered the instrument while we were on Easter Island, but it had taken a side trip to Santiago before Commander Corthron tracked it down, shepherded it through Customs, and personally delivered it to us in Punta Arenas.

When we first had a chance to talk to him, he laughed and told us he was afraid he'd be called out to haul us into port. He and *Colocolo* had towed in the second cruising boat that Admiral Allen mentioned. He also gave us an update on Hal Roth's *Whisper*. She was presently being repaired in Buenos Aires after wrecking her hull on a rock in Rio de la Plata, which must have been an extra blow for the Roths after their earlier shipwreck near Cape Horn.

My immediate focus was assessing *Dolphin*'s repairs. I needed to lodge an insurance claim for damages so we would have money for repairs or whatever we decided to do next. Réanne wanted to let our families know that we were safe. The day after our arrival in Punta Arenas, I wrote to our insurance agent in California, describing the accident and itemizing damages: "*broken spars, rigging, port lights, cracks in deck joints, leaky hull, and ripped sail. Extensive saltwater damage to electronic, radio, and navigation equipment, as well as to our two years' supply of ship's stores. In addition, our dinghy and some deck equipment were lost overboard.*" We continued to find more damage over the next few weeks. When the wind finally dropped for a couple of hours one afternoon in late April, I was able to go up the main mast, where I found that the hardware had all been knocked an inch or more downwards.

When a Chilean Naval engineer completed a formal survey for the insurance report, the list of damages was three pages long. It was hard for us to place a dollar amount on the damages, since we did not know if we could get the materials and equipment in Punta Arenas. Nor could we proceed to a larger port—Valparaiso or Buenos Aires—with the boat in her weakened condition. The Chilean Navy gave us a preliminary estimate of $18,000 for temporary hull repairs, new spars and a rigging refit. With the southern hemisphere winter fast approaching, the alternatives seemed to be to send *Dolphin* home on a freighter or store her in a dry dock until the spring. Neither alternative was acceptable to me, and my frustration mounted.

Meanwhile, *Dolphin* sustained further damage at the Punta Arenas dock as we continually repositioned the boat to protect her from the wild weather. Punta Arenas is an "open roadstead," meaning that instead of an enclosed harbor, there is just a long pier, the *Muelle Pra.* It juts 400 yards out into the Strait of Magellan. *Dolphin* was almost as exposed to the wild conditions tied up to the pier as she had been sailing up the Strait.

Life at the pier was hard on Réanne and me, too. The pier had space for eight ships, four on each side. If more vessels than this were in port at one time, they had to tie alongside one another, or "raft up." Getting to shore from our small boat rafted to the much larger commercial fishing boats required negotiating an obstacle course up and down slippery ladders and over rickety catwalks from boat to boat. All the boats heaved up and down independently, and spurts of water shot up between them as they crashed together in the rough waves.

A log entry from April 9, a few days after our arrival, reported: *Wind today 20-30 knots from southwest. Very rough even on north side of pier. South side would be impossible for little boats. Standing waves off cement bulwarks along shore. Yesterday it was blowing fifty knots from west, with the bay full of white caps and blowing spray.*

Worse, the furious winds changed direction constantly. This meant we could never leave the boat for more than a few hours at a time in case we had to relocate from one side of the pier to the other. The Chilean Navy would alert us whenever such wind shifts occurred, but we had to remain reachable by telephone at all times when we left the boat. Each move was an ordeal, and we more often than not broke something, adding to *Dolphin*'s inventory of damages. Because the pier extended from land in a northwest-southeast direction, winds from either of these directions were not too dangerous; but when the wind blew directly from the north or the south we were in trouble. We had been told that the most frequent winds came from the south, so we tied up initially by ourselves in a space against the north side of the pier. Then a north wind hit at low tide, and while we were trying to get away from the pier—with the help of four sailors—we smashed two lifeline stanchions and the port cathead (the wooden projection at the bow that holds the anchor). Réanne almost got smashed, too. She was trying to help push off and got caught between the huge tire on the side of the pier and the rail. She would have been crushed if I hadn't managed to gun the engine. Much to her embarrassment, she fainted in front of all the sailors, and her abdomen was extremely sore for several days afterwards.

After that experience, I decided to tie up to other boats so we wouldn't get caught against the pier. In that way *Dolphin* would rise with the other boats as the tide rose. This was fine when the wind blew from southeast or northwest. Then we pitched forward and aft, not sideways. But whenever the wind changed, *Dolphin* bobbed around like a cork, bashing her shrouds, toe-rails and catheads against the next boat. At times like that we would have to leave the pier and go out to anchor, and several times we had to keep the motor running to help the anchor keep its hold against the strong winds. Of course, this never seemed to happen in daylight, but only in the middle of the night. At the end of April, Réanne wrote to a friend that we had "Spent five of the past seven days playing ring-around-the-pier, which is a bit much when you're trying to get things done." She and I rarely enjoyed a full night's sleep.

On April 26, a Sunday, a south wind came up at 0400 hours and kicked up six foot waves against the pier. By 0500 hours, we were smashing against the boat beside us, so we got up and went out to anchor, but we had to keep the motor running to help the anchor against the wind. When the sun finally rose at 0800 hours, we followed some fishing boats to a small bay called Bahía Catalina, five miles north of Punta Arenas. The fishermen knew it as the only place offering shelter against the south wind. We anchored there, along with the fishing boats, for three days, until the storm finally abated.

The swells at the dock were still heavy on our return to Punta Arenas, but we needed to tie alongside the dock temporarily so Réanne could get ashore to buy groceries. The wind continued to blow from the south and we were having a hard time getting near enough to the pier to throw up our lines. I threw out a stern anchor as we approached to toss up our mooring lines, but in the process of trying to get close enough I had to put the motor in reverse, and caught the anchor line in the prop. I had no choice but to go in the water and free it after we tied *Dolphin* to the pier. I put on a wetsuit but the water was 35 °F and my feet and head were exposed. It took me almost ten minutes to unsnarl and free the line, by which time my hands and feet were ready to drop off. Réanne had blankets, towels and hot soup waiting when I came out, but I had a pounding headache from the freezing water. An audience of twenty-five to thirty workmen and sailors stood gawking on the dock as I carried out the work. *Loco gringo*!

For all our problems with Punta Arenas as a port, Réanne and I loved the city itself. Réanne wrote to a friend, "if it had a small boat harbor or a floating dock it would be just perfect, but then more people might come." The magic for us lay less in its physical attributes, however, than in the people we met and the friends we made.

Architecturally, Punta Arenas was undistinguished. Still under martial law after Pinochet's coup eighteen months before, the downtown streets were broad and empty, except for the soldiers on most of the street corners. There were few trees, and the buildings were weathered and somewhat dilapidated, though many of the houses and apartments we visited were nice inside. Grey skies added to impression of bleakness, though the sun shone intermittently and the locals would tell us, with a sort of pride, that Punta Arenas was a place with four seasons in one day. The air was cold, but it was also clear and fresh, free of smog or smoke. Réanne and I did a lot of walking, more so after the first week, once our legs got used to the exercise.

Chilean fishermen unloading their catch

*   *   *   *   *

Punta Arenas was a surprising melting pot of nationalities, with many people of British, German, Croatian, and French descent. Though some of them were second and third generation immigrants, many were determined to keep their "mother" language and were bi-lingual. I described Punta Arenas to a state-side friend as being "very international and rather unique—in many ways like a quaint overgrown European village, but with many things going on and a varied mixture of people, tongues, etc."

Along with the mix of cultures came a fantastic variety of food. Though Réanne and I had both lost weight after the pitchpole, we quickly fattened up again on fresh French bread, sweet butter, excellent pastries, homemade empanadas, cheese and fresh meat. Beef, lamb and pork were all cheap in Punta Arenas, as they were locally produced, and Réanne served fantastic pot roasts for forty cents or less a pound. Mussels, scallops, and fish were also plentiful and cheap, but general groceries were expensive. Fresh vegetables were hard to obtain since it was almost winter, although friends occasionally gave us produce from their gardens. Réanne wrote to her parents that she had "dreamed of fresh cauliflower on the ocean and we've had it several times since we arrived."

The locals were all extremely hospitable. On the day we arrived, a director of the local yacht club, Erwin Korn, offered us the use of his washing machine. Humberto Gaete, from the amateur Radio Club asked if we'd like to contact our family in the states. His wife, a teacher at a private English school, wanted to show us around town immediately. We made many friends, as people came down to the pier, introduced themselves, and asked if we would like to come along with them to tea, or for a ride, or for dinner. Our social life was so full that Réanne complained she barely had time to keep up her diary, let alone do any work with me on the boat. I enjoyed the socializing at least as much as she did. While she befriended teachers and visited schools, I collected my own assortment of local characters: a navigator/poet who had repeatedly tried and failed to sail around Cape Horn; the captain of a fisheries research vessel; a man with two wives who was curious to know if American men expected their women to be virgins when they got married.

During our visit, the dictator General Augusto Pinochet ruled Chile, and the Navy in Punta Arenas was under his direct command. Pinochet had come to power a year and a half earlier, in August 1973, after deposing the democratically-elected Socialist president Salvador Allende in a CIA-sponsored coup. A career military officer, Pinochet had been appointed commander-in-chief of the Chilean Army by Allende only eighteen days prior to the takeover. Pinochet was determined to eradicate socialism and re-establish a free-market economy. He sought to crush political dissent, and in his first three years as president, which included the time Réanne and I were in Punta Arenas, some 130,000 people were arrested. Many of these people were tortured, and a number were held as political prisoners in the infamous prison on Dawson Island, across the Strait from Punta Arenas.

In spite of the recent regime change, our Chilean Navy hosts were very gracious to us, as was everyone else we met in Punta Arenas, and we remain thankful to them to this day. However, Punta Arenas was a city under military rule with restrictions on personal liberty that would not have been tolerated in the U.S. Soldiers occupied the streets, and everyone was subject to a nightly midnight curfew. One night Réanne and I enjoyed a late supper at the Savoy Hotel and arrived back at the dock to find twelve armed soldiers there. We did not have our passports with us, but the soldiers let us through while they continued unloading ammunition from a coastal transport ship. There were also military parades through the city every Saturday, with German-trained Chilean soldiers goose-stepping and performing close-arm drills with expert precision. On one Chilean holiday, we flew a United Nations flag from *Dolphin*'s shrouds along with our usual U.S. and Chilean flags while a military parade took place on the pier, generating major frowns from the army officers.

Réanne and I happened to have encountered Pinochet in person in January 1975 during our visit to Easter Island. Easter Island is a Chilean possession, and the new leader flew in to tour the island and inspect the facilities. All government business there had been put on hold in the days before the General arrived, which delayed preparing *Dolphin* for the next leg of our voyage, inconveniencing Réanne and me. Everything and everyone on the island was spruced up. Banners were strung up along the road from the airport welcoming the president and thanking him for having given the island "liberty" and television. When Pinochet finally arrived, he was greeted by both crowds and rain. Bodyguards accompanied the President and his wife, but no guns were in sight, and the people strained to touch him. Visibly gratified by the demonstration of affection, the Pinochets shook hands with every person in a long line, including Réanne and me. We were as excited as everybody else, since we'd never shaken the hand of a dictator before. But we also hoped Pinochet would see our boat and the UN flag flying from the rigging. When the presidential plane took off, it left Pinochet, his wife and guards behind on the island. Someone pointed out to us that if any of them wanted to leave before their plane returned, the only way they could do so was on our boat!

In Punta Arenas, I recounted this episode to the local head of Army intelligence whom Réanne and I met at a party. I have always been anti-military—a character trait that my two-year stint with the US Army in Germany in the early 1950s had failed to eradicate—and I asked the Chilean colonel how he felt about General Pinochet "freeing" Chile. Our host for the evening was furious with us, since he feared he would be held responsible for my indiscretion. However, the colonel remained polite, and when he and I ran into one another again in town we had a drink together. The colonel also arranged for a 50-pound sack of coal to be delivered to us for the stove aboard *Dolphin*, together with a three page propaganda document favorably comparing Pinochet's free-market economic policies with those of his "Marxist" predecessor, Salvador Allende.

For all their hospitality and gracious behavior, the Chilean authorities couldn't help the fact that Punta Arenas had no boat repair facilities that could handle a boat of *Dolphin's* size. Although the *South America Pilot* stated that "Small repairs could be made to larger vessels," it turned out that large repairs to smaller vessels were not possible. It's possible that Punta Arenas has more extensive marine repair facilities nowadays, but in 1975 there wasn't a crane that could lift our twenty-ton boat out of the water. We didn't want to abandon *Dolphin* in Punta Arenas, so somehow we had to get her to a shipyard that could handle the necessary repairs.

Our original itinerary from Los Angeles had included sailing around Cape Horn, then across the Atlantic, via the Falkland Islands and Tristan da Cunha, to Cape Town. Now we were forced to consider other options. One suggestion made to us early in our stay in Punta Arenas was that we load *Dolphin* aboard a Chilean coastal transport vessel to take her to Valparaiso, a thousand miles to the north on Chile's Pacific coast. We could have waited for a freighter with a large enough crane to do the job, but we would also have needed a cradle made to support the boat as she was lifted, and I knew she would take a beating in the process.

In mid-May, a Chilean Navy LST (amphibious landing craft) arrived. Her crew offered to tow us to Puerto Montt, halfway to Valparaiso. The LST was leaving again the next day, so

Réanne and I said yes, and raced excitedly around town, making departure preparations and saying hurried goodbyes to our friends. The local TV station actually reported that we had left, but the announcement turned out to be premature. That same evening, the naval architects who had looked at *Dolphin* to determine the feasibility and mechanics of the tow vetoed the plan as simply too dangerous.

After this, our best option was to complete a few temporary repairs, and then head 1,800 miles north to Buenos Aires, Argentina, where there were facilities for *Dolphin* to undergo a complete overhaul. The weather would be better there too, while in Punta Arenas it was growing colder by the day. A merchant officer from one of the freighters, who had done the Valparaiso to Brazil run for the previous eight years, told us that winter was a favorable time to travel along the Atlantic coastline, either motoring or sailing, because the *pamperos*, the heavy winds that blow off the *pampas* lands of the interior, were not as strong as in summer, and there were generally fewer storms. He suggested that we stay about two miles off the coast—and added, to our great relief, that the seas in the Atlantic were *much* smaller than in the Pacific.

As a sailor and as a man, I have always found it thrilling to speed along, driving my boat and my crew until I achieve maximum performance. My original plan to circumnavigate the southern hemisphere using traditional equipment and old-fashioned seamanship had suffered as much as *Dolphin* had in the rough waters off the coast of southern Chile. The never-ending discomfort and uncertainty also took a toll on my relationship with Réanne. She was sick and tired of the dangerous and uncomfortable living conditions, and she let me know it. At this point, Réanne made it clear that while she understood my desire to continue around the world once *Dolphin* was repaired, she no longer wished to be part of the trip. She agreed that she would help me move *Dolphin* to Buenos Aires if I hired additional crew to assist us. Then she planned to fly back to Los Angeles to continue her teaching career, and be with our youngest son while he finished his last year of high school. I was surprised and distressed by her decision. In my opinion, we had already completed the hardest part of the trip. Her rejection hurt me, and I worried her desertion might thwart the fulfillment of dream.

*   *   *   *   *

In any case, we still had to make whatever boat repairs we could in Punta Arenas. The best place to do this was not actually in Punta Arenas but across the Strait of Magellan on the island of Tierra del Fuego. There we found a small town called Porvenir with a landlocked harbor called Bahía Chilota. Although the winds howled just as strongly as in Punta Arenas (routinely forty-five to sixty-five knots), the protected harbor had no swells, and fishermen took their boats there to work on them.

Bahía Chilota had a narrow, serpentine opening, and we were warned that entering it would be tricky, so we invited my friend from the fisheries research vessel to go along. He guided us successfully into the bay and we rafted alongside a fishing boat at a small pier three miles from Porvenir. The pier served as a landing place for an LST that made daily ferry runs from Punta Arenas to Porvenir. The Navy sent over our mail, telegrams and communications, so we had almost daily door-to-door delivery.

The Porvenir side of Tierra del Fuego was quite dry and flat compared to Punta Arenas, but we found a stark beauty enhanced by dramatic skies. The bay was picturesque, with fishing boats lying beached along the shore and many flocks of ducks and geese. The beaches were heaped with various kinds of shells, since the main local industry was the canning of mussels, clams and king crab, as well as the freezing of lamb and beef.

Our fisheries friend introduced us to his Porvenir associates, including the mayor, who took us on a tour of his town and its environs. The mayor drove us to Lago de los Cisnes where we saw hundreds of flamingos, which arrived every winter. The view was gorgeous—the sun was at just the right angle to light the birds in a panorama of pink, orange and blue. Later in the tour we saw a few black neck swans. The mayor told us the swans usually left in winter while the flamingos had come early. He said that this indicated a long hard winter. We believed him! When we returned to the boat after the tour, the deck was covered with ice from a terrific hailstorm during the afternoon. The hailstones had failed to melt because the ambient temperature was below freezing. Réanne and I nearly broke our necks trying to climb down to *Dolphin* from the fishing boat we were rafted against.

We anchored *Dolphin* at Bahía Chilota just in time to weather a major storm that blew in from the south. In a few hours, the barometer dropped two inches, the wind blew up to Force 6-7 (moderate gale conditions), and we were subjected to a tremendous snow and hail storm that covered the low hills behind Porvenir in white. We heard later that the only other sailboat in the area—a gaff-rigged sloop belonging to the Punta Arenas *Club Nautico*—which had been anchored off the pier, broke its heavy (half-inch) chain in the storm. The boat blew and drifted over sixty miles away before the Navy found it. Fortunately no damage was done, but we could have been in the same situation. Instead, we were snug in Porvenir. The temperature remained below freezing, and we kept the woodstove in the cabin going every night, but we enjoyed our first full nights of sleep for several weeks.

For the next few days, we worked steadily on boat repairs. Our friend at *Club Nautico* recommended a carpenter who made a new mainmast spreader and a staysail boom. He did a great job with these and spliced a new piece onto the main boom. It was a temporary fix, but it would see us through until we arrived at a place where we could have a new boom made. The carpenter also replaced the broken glass in a starboard porthole and made a new cathead for the port bow to replace the original which had ultimately been wrenched out of the deck. We had a six-foot tear in the mizzen staysail sewn up, and on a day when Réanne was away visiting schools in Punta Arenas, I negotiated in "Spanglish" with our fishermen neighbors to reweld *Dolphin*'s broken stanchions. The fishermen also helped us straighten out the self-steering vane which had been bent into a fifteen degree angle. When we finally got a calm day, I went up the mast and reinstalled the spreader. Réanne wrote to our sons that *Dolphin* was "beginning to look like a whole boat again!"

We spent two weeks working on *Dolphin* in Bahía Chilote and Porvenir. I had been anxious to set sail for Buenos Aires around May 10, since this was the only period in the entire month when the tides would be favorable for us to sail through the two sets of narrows in the Strait of Magellan east of Punta Arenas. However, we were still waiting for our insurance settlement, and for our son Jeff to fly down with the electronic equipment (radio, radio direction finder, and depth sounder) we had sent home to the US for repairs. The plan was for Jeff to join us as crew to continue the ongoing voyage. However, a letter arrived from Jeff announcing that he'd decided to stay home, and that the electronics were coming by airfreight. This was a blow in several respects. Had we known earlier, Réanne could have flown home and back with the electronics, or we could have requested that they be sent to us sooner. As it was, we had to impose on Commander Corthron yet again to help us track our box. Réanne wrote to a friend that she had become "an ardent admirer of the capitalist system."

We also knew we needed to find someone to replace Jeff for the voyage to Buenos Aires. As the favorable May tides came and went, and we abandoned the plan to tow *Dolphin* to Valparaiso, we set about in earnest to find additional crew before the next tidal deadline in early June. If we missed the June tides, we would be faced with the unpleasant prospect of being stranded in Punta Arenas until spring.

While we were tied to the *Muelle Prat*, we frequently rafted *Dolphin* to a fishing boat called the *Calabria*. The boat and crew were idled due to lack of money for fuel, and like us, they were not happy to be stuck in Punta Arenas for the winter. We befriended her crew, including a personable young man named Alfonso Bahamonde Díaz. He was twenty-six, single, and without great prospects in Punta Arenas. He expressed interest in coming with us, possibly even as far as California. Alfonso's captain gave him a good recommendation, and as Réanne wrote to her parents, "He even cooks!" A major obstacle was that Alfonso didn't have a passport. Lesser obstacles were that he spoke no English, and he was essentially illiterate, having had almost no formal education. He was told he could apply for passport privileges, but the fee was one million Escudos (about $250). This was a prohibitive sum since Alfonso earned about fifty dollars a month, but we learned a few days later that work and educational sorties were exempt from this fee. We offered him a work contract, which Réanne typed in triplicate for the Chilean officials. It was an old-fashioned seaman's contract that dated back to British sailing ship days. Alfonso signed on to work twenty-four hours a day for seven days a week at my direction. I could fire him anytime, anywhere, but I would have to pay his way back to Punta Arenas. I had Alfonso sign this document in front of Admiral Allen, since I wanted to make sure my new crewman understood his rights and that I was not trying to take advantage of him

.

Dolphin's new crewmember Alfonso Bahamonde

In addition to the seaman's contract, other paperwork included *"solicitudes"* or requests from both Alfonso and us to the Maritime Governor, and to the *Impuestos Internos* bureau (the Chilean equivalent of the IRS), which took three days to prepare. After that, we had to wait for a formal reply from Santiago that cleared Alfonso for passport privileges, at which point his travel documents could be issued in Punta Arenas. Réanne and I found this procedure extremely tedious, but the Chilean officials were always courteous to us, and I was surprised that at no point did any of them ask for "additional remuneration" to speed things up.

While waiting around in Punta Arenas for parts and paperwork, Réanne and I noticed two young backpackers, a man and woman, wandering the streets. They had seen the U.S. flag flying in *Dolphin*'s rigging while they walked along the waterfront, and we finally met them in the coast guard office where they were seeking information about a ferry to Santiago. We stood and chatted for a while, and they told us a bit about their travels. They looked like hippies to me, and I worried that they might be carrying marijuana, so I hesitated to invite them on board *Dolphin*. Discovery of any illegal drugs would have led to seizure of my boat and punishment by Chilean law enforcement. We continued to run into them around town, gradually became better acquainted, and eventually invited them aboard *Dolphin* for tea. Trevor Dwyer was a tall, blonde Englishman in his early thirties. He'd been working a high-stress job as a stage designer for the Nico Milan Opera House in Cape Town, South Africa, and had taken a year off to travel and recover from a painful divorce. Margaret Manzoni was a twenty-year-old redhead. She was a lovely former model for a Cape Town department store and she'd also been studying computer programming while working for Kodak. She was using some of her savings on world travel. The couple had spent ten months rambling and sightseeing around South America and had been stranded in Punta Arenas for several weeks when the ferry to Santiago failed to arrive. Presently living crowded into a backpackers' hostel with a variety of other travelers, including a pair of wanted terrorists from Mozambique, they were eager to leave Punta Arenas before winter really set in.

I looked the pair over carefully. They assured me that they were not drug users, and they seemed fit and capable. Even though they had no sailing experience, their travels indicated that they were adventurous and free spirited. I made up my mind and invited them to join *Dolphin* as part of the crew. Réanne was first astonished and then angry at my impulsive decision, but I didn't see that I had much choice. I still wanted to sail *Dolphin* around the world, and Réanne refused to commit to the voyage. We argued intensely for several days. As Margie later commented, "Long-term couples certainly know how to fight!" However, as Captain, I prevailed, and we prepared *Dolphin* to leave Punta Arenas with five souls aboard.

Margie and Trev continued to spend nights at their hostel, and Alfonso remained aboard the *Calabria* until we were ready to sail. But all three spent their daytime hours aboard *Dolphin* helping with departure preparations. Réanne wrote on May 30: "Fishermen on the boat next door are cutting wood for the trip. Trev is working with Don on some of the lamps— cleaning and rewiring. Margie is mending an Argentine flag." Our three new crewmembers were all cheerful and capable, and I grew increasingly confident that we would work well together.

In the meantime, we were still waiting for our electronics. Although I was determined to use as few electronic aids as possible, *Dolphin* did have a depth sounder, a ham radio, and an intermittently functional tape deck. I had been a ham radio enthusiast since my teenage years, and we were all glad to have this means of communication aboard our small sailboat. We found that while the oceans were huge, amateur radio made the world seem much smaller and friendlier. While at sea, I tried to keep up a nightly ham radio schedule in order to keep in touch with family and friends at home, with my business partners, and with the rest of the world. *Dolphin*'s radio had been destroyed in the pitchpole, but I had ordered a replacement. The new radio was a compact, all solid-state model which I could use to converse with people all over the world. I generally used the 20-meter band frequency, as it had minimal "skip" and interference in the southern hemisphere. Once *Dolphin* reached the Atlantic, I made regular use of a router service that allowed us to make long distance phone patches.

My California business partner telegraphed me that he'd sent the new radio and a replacement depth sounder by air on May 13, but after two weeks the package still had not arrived. I was afraid that the delay meant that all of the equipment had been stolen. On June 3, we heard that a cargo plane was supposed to arrive in Punta Arenas that day, but it failed to do so. In desperation, I had Réanne place a long distance call to the U.S. Embassy in Santiago to see if they could light a fire under someone at the airlines. Whoever she talked to promised to get word to Commander Corthron that same afternoon. The Commander was probably sick and tired of us by then. He was always polite and he had been pretty good at dealing with red tape, but this equipment delay really stumped him. I had decided by then that we would leave by 0500 hours on June 7, even if the equipment failed to arrive. This was the last day for the entire month of June on which the tides through the English Narrows would be favorable. If we didn't leave then we would have to wait another four weeks, or else pay for a tow through the Narrows into the Atlantic Ocean.

On the evening of June 5, Commander Corthron told us he had just received a call from the Naval Attaché at the U.S. Embassy in Santiago saying that the airline had promised the equipment would arrive in Punta Arenas the next day—as indeed it did. The Commander also told us that *Bendoran*, the ship that assisted us during our wild passage to Punta Arenas after the pitchpole, would be arriving sometime the next day, on June 7. Réanne and I had hoped to meet our rescuers again, but I was determined to sail as early as possible on June 7, come hell or high water, so it looked like we would miss them.

Hell arrived, or at least the Punta Arenas version of it. The wind changed to the north just before midnight on June 6, bringing with it a raging snowstorm. *Bendoran* arrived the next morning in the midst of the storm. We raised our British flag and circled the pier so her crew could see us. After completing docking procedures, Captain Addison visited us aboard *Dolphin*, bringing with him another bottle of White Horse whisky. I hadn't met him previously, since I had been too busy filling the diesel jugs to go aboard *Bendoran* in Canal Sarmiento. He invited all five of us to dinner aboard his ship that evening, if we were still in port. He also asked anxiously if he could have *Bendoran's* soup kettle back, since he'd been in trouble with his cook ever since we'd sailed off with it in Canal Sarmiento. We returned the kettle and thanked him again for assisting us. I was sorry to tell him that I planned to leave in the early afternoon.

I thought for a while that we would indeed dine aboard *Bendoran* after all, as Alfonso pulled a typical trick on me. He had gone into town that morning to check on his passport. When he returned, I called to him, "*Passaporto listo?*" "*Lunes*," ("Monday,") he replied. "Monday." Goddammit, today was only Saturday. My whole plan for leaving had just been blown out of the water, and I couldn't tolerate any more frustration. Alfonso kept a straight face for a few minutes. Then he grinned and produced his passport from his pocket. He thought it was hilarious to scare me with bad news that turned out to be a joke.

The next morning, June 7, only the stormy weather delayed our departure. We did some last minute shopping for fresh vegetables and another jug of kerosene, had Chilean exit clearances stamped in our passports, and gave a couple of final newspaper interviews. By mid-afternoon, the wind had swung back to the south, the snow had stopped, and conditions in general had improved. We sent our apologies to Captain Addison and cast off for Buenos Aires.

Réanne and I had made a lot of friends during our two months in Punta Arenas, and fishermen, townsfolk, naval officers, and tourists all grouped together on the dock waving, ringing bells, and shouting goodbye. In spite of the sadness that comes with farewells, we were relieved and excited to leave Punta Arenas at last. We headed out in the late afternoon sunlight with a moderate south breeze. Grey and white dolphins with smiling faces surfed alongside *Dolphin* in the clear water— Margie observed that the boat was well-named indeed, and I reminded the crew that sailors have always considered dolphins to be good omens.

Chapter 4

Punta Arenas, Chile to Buenos Aires,

Argentina

7 June - 9 July, 1975

My goal that first afternoon after leaving Punta Arenas was to sail for a few hours to a small harbor called Cabo Negro so we could anchor before nightfall. I wanted to start our trip with a simple "shake-down" cruise so the new crew could get a feeling for boat handling and sail trim, and start learning their general responsibilities. Margie had never sailed before and she confessed to a little anxiety. I showed her how to steer and left her sitting alone for a while at the helm. She carefully kept the compass heading and looked completely relaxed, as if she'd been sailing a twenty-ton ketch through the wilds of the Strait of Magellan all her life.

We dropped anchor in the cove of Cabo Negro at 1930 hours on Saturday, June 7. The flash of the lighthouse on Isla Magdalena, a small island we planned to explore in the morning, beamed from the headland. After enjoying our first dinner together as boat mates, we chatted for an hour and went to bed. I awoke just before dawn the next morning. The temperature had dropped considerably from the day before and the wind had a biting chill. A light dusting of snow coated the deck, although the rising sun revealed a clear blue sky and the frost rapidly disappeared. In the distance we could see the silhouette of Isla Magdalena. We pulled up the anchor and set a course across a massive tidal rip for the lee side of the island. A distinctive dark line along the island's cliffs revealed the twenty-four foot difference between low and high tide.

Just after 0900 hours, we arrived at the northwest corner of the island. Alfonso stayed on board as anchor watch, and the rest of us went ashore in the dinghy I'd bought in Punta Arenas to replace the one lost in the pitchpole. We landed on a pebble beach and set off toward the center of the island. As we climbed up the slopes we found hundreds of penguin nests and the corpses of numerous Magellanic penguins scattered about on the ground. We found just one live bird. All of the others had already headed north to warmer weather, leaving behind the weak and the young. Each summer, an estimated 60,000 pairs of Magellanic penguins nest in a single large community on the highest part of the island, making it one of the largest penguin colonies in southern Chile. When the penguins return each December, they lay their eggs on top of mud mounds dug from the clay, and sit on them until they hatch. Their excavations were like rabbit holes, forming a warren of underground tunnels and chambers that sometimes collapsed underfoot, making walking extremely tricky. Each of us sank to the knees several times.

In earlier times, Isla Magdalena had been home to more than penguins. At the top of the slopes, where the land leveled out, loose stones had been piled up to form a rough wall. We imagined Indians crouching behind it to hunt penguins and shelter from the constant winds. Nearby, away from the wall, we found man-made depressions where the Indians had slept, and smaller depressions where they'd made fires. Presumably, the Indians had done their cooking and eating here, as discarded penguin bones were strewn about. Trev found a stone arrowhead, setting off a frenzy of excited searching. We found no other artifacts, although I spotted some obsidian chips that must have been imported by Indians, since there was no local obsidian. The arrowhead could have been hammered out by either one of the two tribes of canoe Indians, the Alakaluf or the Yahgan, whom Magellan had discovered inhabiting the land and channels in the Strait when he sailed through it in 1520. Today, these tribes are almost extinct.

Exploring the penguin mounds of Isla Magdalena

Isla Magdalena is home to the old lighthouse whose flash we had seen the night before from Cabo Negro. Built in 1901, it sits at the top of a loose-stoned cliff, and we scrambled up to explore it. The light had been automated several decades earlier, so the adjacent light-keeper's house was empty, but the door of the lighthouse was unlocked and we went in and up a drafty, rickety staircase to the working part of the building. At the top, we found a classic Fresnel lens. As an engineer, I appreciated it as a masterpiece of functional design. Named for its inventor, the French physicist, Augustin Jean Fresnel, the Fresnel lens is brilliantly simple in concept, thinner and lighter than the equivalent spherical lens. Imagine taking a magnifying glass and slicing it into a series of concentric rings. Each ring is slightly thinner than the next and focuses the light toward the center. Flatten each on one side, stack the rings back together, and you have a Fresnel lens. The lens of the Isla Magdalena lighthouse is approximately ten feet high and about six feet wide. The light, which can be seen for ten miles out to sea, still operates today.

*   *   *   *   *

We had satisfied our exploring instincts for the day, and the turning tide and rising wind warned us to return to *Dolphin*. A few dolphins accompanied us as we rowed back, and the aroma of freshly baked bread wafting from the boat enticed us. Alfonso turned out to have a talent for baking bread! We were ravenous and appreciated his offering. Margie and Réanne sliced tomatoes and cheese, opened a jar of olives and a bottle of Chilean red wine, and we enjoyed a light meal before pulling up the anchor and continuing eastward through the Strait of Magellan. As the evening grew dark, we could see fires burning on both sides of the Strait. Magellan had named the southern shore *Tierra del Fuego*—Land of Fire—because he saw many Indian fires burning there. In 1975, the name was still appropriate, although the fires we saw were flares from oil and gas wells.

It took us the next five days to transit the Strait of Magellan from Punta Arenas to Punta Dungeness and Cabo Virgenes and then out into the Atlantic Ocean. I was pleased with how quickly we settled into a routine. Trev and Alfonso took alternating four-hour watches at night, and the girls and I relieved at them at the helm during the day. Réanne and Margie shared the cooking, with occasional help from Alfonso, and they kept the helmsmen supplied with hot drinks. As the captain, I was in charge of navigation and responsible for all decisions on board. I was always "on call," whatever the time of day. I also made entries in the logbook almost hourly, noting wind and sea conditions, sail changes, and anything else that related to the functioning of the boat. *Dolphin*'s chronometer was set to Greenwich Mean Time, but the actual time of day was irrelevant. Our stomachs and body clocks ruled. Like the birds of the air, we slept during the darkness and awoke with the first rays of sunlight. The helmsmen took their night watches, and steered us safely to each new morning.

*   *   *   *   *

Even with five of us aboard, there was always plenty to do, but everybody was cheerful, cooperative and responsible. We were all getting along quite well, and Réanne thought that Trev, in particular, was a good influence on me because he never got ruffled. He just took everything with relentless good humor. As we became better acquainted, Alfonso's nickname became Alfie. He was an uneducated man with a pleasant personality. He spoke almost no English, although he soon learned plenty of expletives. *Dolphin* had bunks for six. Alfie generally slept in the portside quarter berth. Réanne and I liked the three-quarter bunk in the main cabin, and Trev and Margie shared the aft berth. We were never more than ten or fifteen feet from one another for the entire voyage, and there wasn't much privacy, especially when we were at sea. As the saying goes, "there are no secrets on a boat," but nobody seemed to mind sharing the cramped space. The small wood-burning stove in the main cabin supplied all the heat, so some space had to be devoted to fuel storage. The galley had a two-burner kerosene stove and oven mounted on gimbals to minimize the motion from the rolling seas. Réanne taught Margie and Alfie the techniques for using the stove and oven, and all three were adept at turning out delicious meals and treats, including cakes. *Dolphin* had no refrigeration, since I thought that was just asking for trouble. A fridge would just break down and become a useless object taking up valuable space in our small living quarters.

As we neared the Atlantic, the seas got choppier and a heavy swell set in. The boat pitched and rolled uncomfortably and cross currents flowing from the Atlantic into the Strait hampered maneuverability. We got caught by a gale between the first and second narrows and spent the night anchored in a kelp patch. The next morning, Alfie and Trev battled to control the wheel as we rounded Cabo Virgenes and entered the waters of the open Atlantic. Even with the engine running at full capacity, it took us four hours to cover a distance of two miles. We anchored on several more nights after this, to wait out the weather and maintain crew morale, as Réanne, Margie and Alfie were all suffering from bouts of seasickness. The wind blew between Force 3 and 5, (from seven to twenty-one knots), bringing hail along with almost constant rain, fog, and near-freezing temperatures. In spite of the wintry conditions, sea birds

swarmed among the rocks, including crested rock hopper penguins.

I set *Dolphin*'s course to parallel the coast fairly closely even after we left the Strait of Magellan. The farthest we deliberately ventured offshore into the Atlantic Ocean was thirty miles. In addition to the sails, we motored most of the time in order to maintain a minimum boat speed of at least five knots. I wanted to get north of the "Screaming Fifties" as fast as we could. Visibility was often just a mile in the fog and rain, and only the depth sounder kept us from disaster. The coast was armored with rocks and reefs, and strong counter currents and opposing winds challenged navigation. It could have been worse. As Réanne wrote to a friend, "The seas were choppy, which made the boat uncomfortable, but it was nothing like that damn Pacific!"

On June 12, sailing north and hugging the Patagonian shore for protection from the gale-force westerly wind, we crossed the 50°S parallel. I broke out Captain Addison's White Horse Scotch and drank toasts to the Screaming Fifties, the boat, Réanne, the crew, and Captain Addison himself. We were now sailing in the Roaring Forties. But what an initiation, with ice on deck, huge and erratic swells, "confused seas," and intolerable wind chill. We were freezing even though we were all wearing foul weather gear, including waterproof oil-skinned trousers and jackets.

I couldn't believe Réanne, Margie, and Alfie were still feeling seasick.

"You guys are a bunch of slackers," I told them. "This is great sailing weather! Get your heads in the game—there's no such thing as seasickness."

"I'll show you seasickness," said Margie. "Come a little closer and I'll upchuck on your boots!"

After hours of struggling into the gusty wind and wild current, I spotted a little bay on the chart called Bahía Laura, where I decided to seek shelter until weather conditions improved. This was no easy task. According to the chart, there should have been a lighthouse on the northern cliffs, but I couldn't see it in the poor visibility and rough conditions. *Dolphin* crept forward almost blindly under power while Réanne and Margie read the depths off the echo sounder. Once safely anchored, we enjoyed a good night's sleep in calmer waters without the noise of the diesel.

We woke the next morning to see cliffs only fifty feet in front of us. Had we run into them in the dark, *Dolphin* would have been battered to bits, and we'd all have been killed. I decided we should wait out the storm that day, which was Friday, June 13. Since I was born on a Friday the thirteenth, it's always been my lucky day. This was another lucky day: we hadn't met disaster against the rugged cliffs. We lit a fire in the cabin stove and attempted to dry our clothing, while baking some potatoes for lunch. In the afternoon the sun peeked through the clouds and we had an early dinner outside in the cockpit. I reasoned that with the wind still blowing strongly outside our cove, we should spend a second night anchored right where we were. The ailing crew needed a little more time to find their sea legs, and I wasn't eager to continue in the dark if other lighthouses weren't operational.

When we set out again, I was relieved to spot the next light at Puerto Deseado. As we continued up the coast, I asked a ham radio contact in the U.S. to report several non-functioning lights to the Argentine authorities so the lights could either be repaired or the nautical charts updated. This information was essential for any vessel sailing in these waters, though few sailed as close to the coast as we did. Most vessels stayed in the shipping lanes, farther out to sea.

New to sailing, Margie had a lot of questions about my navigational strategy.

"Why don't we just turn east and head out to sea? We could sail without constantly tracking our depth, and not worry about all these invisible lighthouses. And we wouldn't be panicking about uncharted reefs."

"I want to stay close to shore," I told her. "Since we aren't getting any weather reports, we may need more of these little inlets for shelter."

Margie wasn't satisfied. "Wouldn't it be faster with a steadier wind, away from all these cliffs?"

"Sailing in the offshore wind and waves would be more exciting, and we might make better time, but the seas out there get rough fast. Staying near the coast gives us some options for protection, and we can always anchor for a while if we get tired."

Privately, I was also concerned about the sturdiness of *Dolphin*'s temporary repairs, so I wanted to avoid the rougher conditions of the open ocean without raising anyone else's fears. Staying near shore also meant that I didn't have to rely on time-consuming celestial navigation observations and computations to determine our position every day; I could figure it out by taking bearings on the landmarks like capes, islands, and lighthouses, along the shore. What we were doing, in fact, was what is known among cruising sailors as "gunkholing"—cruising close to shore and spending most nights in sheltered anchorages. (The "gunk" part of the term comes from the gunk, or mud, characteristic of creek estuaries and shallow water.)

On June 16, we crossed the 45°S parallel, surfing down the troughs of huge waves and crossing giant rip currents on the way. We finally had our first really fair sailing winds, blowing up from the south. I wrote in the log that we were "screaming along" under mainsail alone, traveling fifty miles in ten hours. Alfie was beginning to appreciate sailing on *Dolphin*. With a big grin, he told me, "She likes a lot of wind!" We anchored that night in a place called Punta Glora. The sheep on the shore were the first life we'd seen on land since leaving Punta Arenas. The coastline was incredibly desolate, a brown shore with no vegetation, just stark sand and occasional weird sandstone formations. Cruising and anchoring along this wild coast was gunkholing at its finest!

Out at sea, it was a different story. Black and white dolphins continued to accompany us when we were sailing, and every now and then an albatross would soar overhead. Réanne and I had seen wandering albatrosses on the South Pacific leg of our voyage. The first one showed up south of Easter Island, and we saw many more after we pitchpoled. Albatrosses were my favorite birds. I was entranced by their flying abilities and wrote about them in my ship's log: "Most magnificent animals. No zoo on Earth could show what beautiful and splendid skill and grace these fine birds have. Their lone treks and flying skills are truly beyond description." I sketched them as well, but failed to do them justice. They soared alongside for hours, swooping and swerving without ever flapping their wings. The engineer in me appreciated the locking mechanism in their wings that allows them to glide without tiring. Humans have yet to design wing structures that can even come close to what these birds can do with wind-power alone. In dynamic soaring mode, they rise and descend repeatedly into the wind, gaining energy from the vertical wind gradient without having to flap their wings. They also practice slope soaring, using the rising air on the windward side of large waves.

In calm weather, albatrosses sometimes have to rest on the surface of the water until the wind picks up again. Their need for wind is one reason they tend to be found more often in the higher latitudes, rather than the equatorial "doldrums." I never grew tired of watching them.

The others joked that the albatross was only with us for the music. Trev had tinkered with our tape deck to get it working again. Over the noise of the wind, the two speakers on deck blasted out Crosby, Stills, and Nash, Jim Croce, Kris Kristofferson, John Denver, and Cat Stevens. Réanne had some classical tapes, but our young crew preferred the more contemporary music, and I did too.

As we moved along, Trev suddenly hollered, "Fish on the line!" Great news—now we'd have fresh tuna for lunch! There was nothing like eating a freshly caught and filleted fish clean from the ocean, and we still had enough fresh ingredients left to make a salad to go with it. Befitting a crewman from a fishing boat, Alfie had many ways of preparing fish: battered and fried, grilled, or dried for later use. He was particularly resourceful at making the fish last for a few days without refrigeration: on Day Three, whatever was left would go into a broth and then we'd enjoy fish soup for a day or two.

*   *   *   *   *

As we headed north along the Argentine coast toward Puerto Madryn, the wind rose to Force 6, or twenty-two to twenty-seven knots. I had the crew raise all the working sails, and we surged along although I remained concerned about *Dolphin*'s overall strength in heavy conditions. The harder we sailed, the more effort the crew had to put into emptying the bilges. At times, all five of us were topside, taking bearings on coastal headlands, adjusting sails, and reading depths off the echo sounder. I tried to follow the twenty-fathom line as much as possible. It was concentrated work, physically and mentally. The weather remained cold and a light rain had set in, limiting visibility. The last night before we reached Puerto Madryn, we took refuge overnight in a little bay called Punta Ninfas. The lighthouse wasn't working, and we had to battle a strong ebbing tide and some current rips. My logbook recorded it as a "cracker anchorage," surrounded on three sides by sheltering cliffs. The logbook added, "Scotch, music, and peanuts for two hours to unwind!"

On the evening of June 18, black and white dolphins escorted us into Puerto Madryn, our first port of entry in Argentina. We had a wild time locating the harbor entrance in the rainy darkness and finally anchored at half past midnight. Puerto Madryn lies at 43°S, exactly ten degrees north of Punta Arenas, and the weather was correspondingly warmer. Once anchored, we made a fire in the cabin stove and then nearly stifled in the heat. Although it was 50 °F outside, it seemed like the tropics! We listened to tapes, ate the last can of peanuts, and sipped hot chocolate or the last of *Bendoran*'s whisky to celebrate our arrival. For the first time since mid-February, Réanne was not wearing her long underwear. Margie complained about the inconvenience of no refrigeration for the butter, cheese and meat, but we were all relieved to have left the chill of the far south behind us.

The next morning, we raised the quarantine flag on *Dolphin*'s rigging. This square yellow flag is also known as the "yellow jack." All vessels arriving from foreign ports are required to display it, with no one allowed on or off the vessel until arrival procedures have been completed. Réanne and I headed into the Puerto Madryn port office to officially check in. We planned to refuel here, and if the weather and port conditions were good enough, I thought we might stay a few days. Puerto Madryn was little more than a village at the time, and notable mostly for its fifteen foot tidal range. At low tide, we had a daunting climb up a rusty thirty-foot high ladder to reach the wharf.

Réanne had written to the Puerto Madryn port officials from Punta Arenas, telling them of our arrival date, crew aboard, and documentation. We expected a cordial and efficient check-in, but it didn't turn out that way. We were ushered into a drab cubicle with ten foot high ceilings, mustard yellow paint peeling off the walls, a single light bulb hanging from a frayed cord in the center of the room, and one small window letting in a dim beam of light. A young corporal in Fidel Castro uniform with a cigar hanging from the side of his mouth was sitting at the desk. He looked at us without expression, and said nothing. Réanne explained that we had just arrived from Chile on our yacht and that we wished to sign in. He turned and asked a man in civilian clothes what he should do. Together, the two of them began looking through a thick manual. Neither acknowledged our presence in the slightest. After we had waited for ten minutes, Réanne and I took out our diaries and began writing in them, a trick that sometimes helps hasten the *tramites* (a useful Spanish word that covers anything from procedural paperwork to bureaucratic hassles).

Réanne eventually asked Fidel if he had received the letter from Punta Arenas advising of our arrival. "*Sí, sí, sí,*" he replied. Then little by little, with time out to refer to certain pages of the manual, we saw action. Our passports and crew lists were finally stamped, though Fidel still offered no information. The crew list read as follows:

- ∞ Don Douglass: Captain, Owner, Navigator
- ∞ Réanne Douglass: First Mate, Writer, Wife
- ∞ Margaret Manzoni: Cook, Photographer
- ∞ Trevor Dwyer: Helmsman, Repairman
- ∞ Alfonso Bahamonde: Helmsman, Fisherman, Baker

Réanne asked if we needed to report back to the Prefectura before our departure to get the transit paperwork (the *zarpe*) required for foreigners traveling in Argentina. "*Sí, sí, sí,*" answered young Fidel.

"What do you need to see? Should we bring the copy of the crew list back? Is there any time of the day or night we can't report?" asked Réanne.

"No, no. We are open twenty-four hours a day."

"Okay, great. We'll check out in a day or two."

We left the office relieved, but a little concerned about our lack of a *zarpe*. That night we all went out for dinner. The waiter was attentive and on his recommendation we ordered *bife complete* (steaks with vegetables, salad, bread, dessert, and coffee) and a carafe of red wine. The whole meal, with a four-piece orchestra accompaniment, was ridiculously cheap, the equivalent of eight U.S. dollars for all five of us. We were certainly celebrating—we all felt that we'd accomplished something by sailing along that treacherous coastline.

Early the next morning, the girls set out to buy supplies for the next leg of our voyage. Margie went in search of fresh bread and told us about the little baker she'd found.

"This place is just a village with no real bakery," she reported later. "The grocer told me to go down three streets to the house with a blue fence. He said the lady there, Grandma Liliana, sells bread sometimes. I found the house, and a little round lady answered the door. She didn't speak any English at all, but I did a little mime, and she figured out that I wanted some bread. I got three loaves for five pesos. After I paid her, I gave her a Kennedy silver half-dollar, and she kissed me on both cheeks!"

On her way back, Margie caught up with Réanne who was walking back to the boat with two large boxes of supplies. Margie took one box, and balanced the bread on top. A man on a bicycle skidded to a stop to let them cross the street, but then he pointed out that they weren't sharing the load evenly. He offered to take the bread for them in his front basket. The girls didn't trust him, and he rode off swearing at them. The rude encounter couldn't spoil their fine day ashore, since both girls were happy to be back on dry land.

By the time Réanne and Margie arrived back at the pier, we men were sweaty and dirty from loading water, kerosene, and diesel fuel on board. A pistol-toting soldier came down to the dock and demanded that we raise the Argentine flag. I hadn't realized it was Argentina's Flag Day, a national holiday. Trev promptly hoisted the flag, and I was glad Margie had finished mending it back in Punta Arenas. We stowed our respective purchases quickly, and decided to clean up at the yacht club and go to the movies in honor of the holiday. We saw *The Gods Must be Crazy*, a Botswanan comedy that our South African crewmembers particularly enjoyed, and all of us identified with the offbeat characters experiencing adventures just like we were on *Dolphin*. Later that evening, Trev, Alfie, and I visited a Greek fishing boat that was tied up next to us. It had been impounded by the Argentine naval authorities 215 miles offshore for allegedly fishing in "Argentine waters." Argentina was proving to be a challenging place for foreigners.

By our third morning in Puerto Madryn, we were prepared for our five day cruise to the city of Mar del Plata, which lies about 300 miles south of Buenos Aires. I wished Réanne luck, and crossed my fingers as she went back to the port office to check out before our departure. She presented the officers with all our documents and the required crew list, and got a similarly nonchalant response to our casual check in.

"We'd like to leave this afternoon," she said. "What should I do to sign out?" She asked three different bureaucrats, none of whom could give her an answer.

Finally, a man in a khaki-colored uniform poked his face out the door and said, "No problem, just go."

"Doesn't someone need to sign our crew list? We still don't have our *zarpe*, and I'm sure we need one."

"No, no, just leave. It's no problem."

A sailor on the pier helped us cast off, and in full view of the *Prefectura* we raised sail, and said *adiós* to Puerto Madryn.

We made good time flying the genoa. Although we encountered huge tidal rips, strong and fair winds carried us north. Conditions for the first couple of days were almost ideal, and the susceptible crew members started to recover from their seasickness. The pleasant conditions let Margie and Trev enjoy the selection of books we had on board. Although we'd thrown away a lot of the books that had been damaged in our pitchpole accident, *Dolphin* still had a sizeable library, with authors ranging from Tolstoy to Paul Hogan ("Crocodile Dundee"). The rhythmic lapping of the waves and the rocking movement of the boat made it hard for the helmsmen to maintain alertness in the chilly night watches. Keeping warm was essential, but it was counter-productive to staying awake. The key was coffee and cookies, and Margie even managed to bake an apple pie.

Adding to my contentment, Réanne was enjoying this leg of the voyage as much as any time we had spent at sea since we set out from Los Angeles. This was in spite of the rough weather and her occasional queasiness. She appreciated having other people along to share the hard work of sailing—hauling in the anchor line, raising and lowering sails, pumping the bilges, and so forth. I was also glad to have the extra help. The congenial and hard working crew and the improving weather led me to hope that Réanne might rethink her decision to abandon the trip after we reached Buenos Aires. Maybe she would continue with the rest of us from there, after we had undertaken the necessary boat repairs. Alfie had told me before we left Punta Arenas that he thought he would sail all the way to California with me, whichever route we took. Trev's ultimate goal was to find work in Hollywood set design, and as he and Margie grew accustomed to life at sea, they decided that working their passage on *Dolphin* was a fine way to travel to California. As the days progressed, we discussed sailing north to Brazil, across the Atlantic to Europe, and maybe even reviving my original plan and sailing all the way around the world. Things were looking up.

The wind strengthened as we pushed up the coast toward our next stop, Mar del Plata. The current was against us, the ride was bouncy and uncomfortable, and Réanne, Alfie, and Margie all got seasick again. The increasing wind and waves made *Dolphin* leak faster, so everyone had to take turns at the bilge pump, regardless of seasickness. I had all the working sails up—main, mizzen and working jib—but I became concerned that the force of the wind might overtax *Dolphin's* temporary repairs so I ordered them lowered. The wind continued to increase up to Force 10, or forty-eight to fifty-five knots. In the next thirty hours, this *pampero*, a blast of cold dry air from the *pampas* or Argentine prairies, carried us from about a mile offshore to 150 miles out to sea. The only safe strategy was to drop *Dolphin's* sails, turn tail, and run with the storm, since the wind and waves would probably continue to worsen before they eased. Réanne was too sick to help, but the others were able to assist with storm preparations. Alfie took the helm, although he was dry heaving. We made sure the forward hatch was battened down and all sail bags and other loose objects on the foredeck—the dinghy, a drum of diesel fuel—were securely tied.

We were carried further and further out to sea and the waves continued to grow, reaching thirty feet high. Wild foam

Trev steering *Dolphin* in the South Atlantic

drove across the deck as *Dolphin* bounced and rolled. We all found it difficult to keep our feet, and I made sure we all had safety harnesses secured to the jacklines around the rails. Alfie stood his watches in spite of constant dry-heaving. He also took the extra precaution of wearing his life vest.

I had learned how to rig *Dolphin* for heavy weather conditions while sailing from Easter Island to the Strait of Magellan, and now it was time to set the equipment up again. Trev and I readied a warp, a long, heavy rope cleated to the stern, with a chain-wrapped tire at the far end. The drag from the warp would help control *Dolphin*'s direction and speed, keeping her stable as she surfed down the wind-driven waves, preventing her from going too fast and possibly broaching (turning sideways and rolling over) or pitchpoling. We threw the tire out on a 400-foot line. In the howling wind, it bounced across the surface of the water until the line grew taut. The tire sank but the resistance it offered was not enough. Our speed continued to increase in the gale. An hour later, we let out a second warp. We had more chain on this one and it helped immediately. Our speed slowed and the boat seemed to stabilize a little.

There was nothing we could do but run before the winds and rolling seas until the *pampero* blew itself out. The seasick crew had day and a night of misery as we surfed down the waves, but I was exhilarated by the wild ride. We were over a hundred miles out to sea after twenty-four hours of gale-force winds. We were also in the middle of the shipping lanes, though not by choice. We saw lights from other vessels to the north and I instructed Alfie to steer well away from them. I was asking a lot of my crew in those conditions, but they had to believe I was making the right decisions, whether to continue running with the wind, or to tack. I kept my fears about Dolphin's repairs to myself, and had faith that she would hold together. Pumping the bilges was almost a full time job, just as it had been off the coast Chile after the pitchpole.

Conditions hadn't improved by daylight, but I was able to assess the storm's damage. All the internal kerosene lamps had been extinguished; the fresh water pump at the galley sink was jammed in an upright position; a wicker basket holding a cask of wine had broken apart so the floor was slippery with red Chilean wine; onions and oranges rolled around; and an upended tray of fudge added to the gooey mess. In addition, one of the engine batteries had boiled over. I couldn't find a workable bandwidth on the radio transmitter so we were completely cut off from the rest of the world. Although the cabin floor was covered with a sloshing mess of garbage, *Dolphin* hadn't sustained any substantial damage.

Réanne and Margie were still throwing up intermittently, and they had terrible headaches. Alfie continued to dry heave, but he had never once stopped to lie down in the previous thirty hours. I was grumpy and exhausted after sleeping only thirty minutes for the past two days. Adding insult to injury, I got "pooped" (smacked) by a wave that came over the stern as I attempted to take a sun shot in the cockpit. Irritation mounted as strain and fatigue took their toll on the crew. Trev remained positive, even as he and I, having failed to unjam the water pump, tried to fill a one-gallon water jug from a five-gallon plastic container. Réanne told me it was like watching a bad Italian movie of two drunk men trying to pour liquid from one container to another on unstable legs.

At 2300 hours on June 24, the wind suddenly dropped. I called the crew up on deck to set up the sails for the tack that would carry *Dolphin* to Mar del Plata. The South American *Coast Pilot* recommended that vessels stay fifteen miles away from the Valdez Peninsula, a large headland north of Puerto Madryn. The pampero had blown us safely past, and now *Dolphin* could turn and head directly for Mar del Plata. Even though we were well out of sight of land, we could see the glow of lights from the coastal towns reflecting off the clouds at night. The technical name for this reflection is lume; it is also called skyglow. Alfie had never sailed out of sight of land before, and he had a tendency to steer toward the lights on shore, rather than following our actual course. When I came up at 0300 hours, I sighted land in the distance. Alfie sheepishly admitted to heading straight toward shore during his watch. He was really nervous when we were out of sight of land.

Excitement reigned as we approached Mar del Plata late that night. The full moon and stars shone overhead as four dolphins played in our bow wave in the calm seas. The city lights were welcoming and our mood was light and happy. The whole crew came up on deck at dawn. We enjoyed hot chocolate and toast together, laughing and chatting, pleased with outlasting the *pampero*.

Dolphin entered the harbor of Mar del Plata on the afternoon of June 25, 1975, sailing the last stretch parallel to a beautiful surf beach. Keeping a watchful eye on the backs of the large breakers crashing onto the sand, I steered through a narrow entrance into the sheltered harbor. The depth sounder read only two meters, but an old man in a small blue dinghy directed us by hollering in English through a megaphone. "Take it easy, *amigos*!" I learned later that this reassuring sentence was the only English he knew. He indicated that we should follow him to the yacht club in the inner basin. His name was Atilio and he was adept at rowing from a standing position, facing his destination and using both oars to push his little dinghy forward through the water.

From the dock, Réanne and I were escorted to the *Prefectura* office by an armed guard, while the crew headed for hot showers at the yacht club. Since the authorities in Puerto Madryn had failed to issue our *zarpe*, we were immediately subjected to a barrage of questions.

"Where is your *zarpe*? It's illegal to voyage in Argentina without a *zarpe*! Who signed you out of Puerto Madryn? What did he look like? What color uniform was he wearing? How many stripes did he have on his shirt? Didn't you know it was illegal to leave without permission?" We spent three hours at the *Prefectura* waiting for them to decide what to do with us. We offered to leave the country. "Oh no, that won't be necessary. We will write to Puerto Madryn to ask for their side of the story. You come back tomorrow."

Approaching and entering the *Prefectura* was a real challenge. There were no sidewalks, but six inches of rainwater flooded the pavement, and an armed guard pointed his gun at us, forcing us to wade through the puddles. "Let's hit the pedestrian" seemed to be the favorite game of the Argentine drivers. Machine gun batteries stood at every corner, with the guns aimed along the streets. When we returned to the office the next day, the guard frisked me and searched Réanne's handbag. We put up with more questions from the men in the front office before they transmitted the message to *Señor* Rodriguez, the official whom we were supposed to see. After another hour wait, we offered to come back the next day. "Oh, no, that won't be necessary, *Señor* Rodriguez will be here in a minute."

Thirty minutes later, *Señor* Rodriguez appeared and apologized, saying, "I'm sorry, I always have so many papers to do." Then immediately he sent for an interpreter. After fifteen more minutes, the interpreter arrived. I explained the whole story to him in English, and he told me that we needed an interpreter who understood more English than he did. We waited another thirty minutes—why not? We'd already missed the appointment that the *Prefectura* had set up for us at the fuel dock. A second interpreter arrived. It was now past lunchtime and we'd arrived at the office early in the morning, without eating breakfast. We explained the whole story for the fourth time. In the meantime, Réanne had a chance to read the exit forms forwarded from Puerto Madryn. They were nothing but lies! The second interpreter told *Señor* Rodriguez that he was inclined to believe our story, but *Señor* Rodriguez told us that we had to go through the official channels. He smiled and said, "At the most, it will cost you twenty dollars." This made me furious! I had never paid a bribe in my life, and I refused to start there. Réanne told me to keep my mouth shut or it would cost us three times as much. Finally, Réanne and I each wrote separate depositions that described our experiences in Puerto Madryn. The interpreter translated them into Spanish (correctly), and we signed them. We were told to return the next day to hear the final decision.

When we returned to the yacht, I was so spitting mad that I wrote a letter of protest to the Chief of the *Prefectura* saying that I had sailed 10,000 miles without encountering difficulty and that I had been cited by the Chilean Navy as worthy of emulation by their naval cadets. I felt the *Prefectura* of Puerto Madryn was being unethical, and that they should demand better service from their officers. All of the different officials told different stories, trying to make me pay for their inefficiency and possible malfeasance.

When we returned to the *Prefectura* again the next day, I presented a copy of my letter to the front desk to be taken to *Señor* Rodriguez. While we sat and waited in the lobby, an officer's .45 pistol fell out of his holster and onto the floor, spilling bullets everywhere. I figured I could get to the gun first, knock its owner on the head, and take charge. The idea was very tempting, but I undoubtedly would have been shot. I was frustrated with the whole situation, and I had no intention of paying the officers any money.

Eventually, *Señor* Rodriguez and the interpreter came into the room. The interpreter had obviously been trying to smooth the waters. He said, "I understand you perfectly well. Your sense of justice as a mariner has been offended, but we think it is better not to make a record of your letter."

Señor Rodriguez said "*Si, si*, the *Jefe* (Chief) has recommended to the *Prefectura* in Puerto Madryn that your case be judged a matter of 'misunderstanding due to language.' We will contact them again for your *zarpe*. You must stay here in Mar del Plata and check in at my office every morning until the correct papers arrive from Puerto Madryn."

I looked at Réanne and whispered out of the side of my mouth, "Do we accept?"

"Yes, for heaven's sake, let's get this over with, otherwise we'll be here fighting ever." I agreed. We all shook hands, smiles on everyone's face. All the papers were sent to Puerto Madryn for re-examination, and we promised to check in every morning.

Mar del Plata is the second largest city in Argentina after Buenos Aires. In 1975, it was clean, with freshly painted buildings and the atmosphere of an affluent seaside town. After checking in at the *Prefectura* each morning, we spent relaxing days exploring the city streets, boutiques, and markets, and absorbing the atmosphere of the place and the vibrant Argentine culture. We found markets offering fresh fruits and street vendors selling tasty hamburgers. There were museums of art and music. Sport was popular too. A huge poster of Guillermo Vilas, a highly ranked Argentine tennis player of the 1970s, dominated the entrance to the *barrio* (street market area). Posters advertising an upcoming boxing match between Muhammad Ali and Joe Bugner adorned street poles everywhere.

We watched the Ali-Bugner fight televised live from Malaysia on June 30 at the home of a clothing merchant named Carlos. He and his wife, Marcella befriended Réanne and Margie when they shopped in his store in central Mar del Plata. Carlos and Marcella invited us to watch the fight with them, and they entertained all five of us in grand style, with spicy grilled chicken, salads, and plenty of strong Argentine wine. We all cheered for Ali, who won his fight.

During our stay in Mar del Plata, we were frequently invited into other people's homes. We men could arrive in jeans and T-shirts, but Réanne and Margie felt they needed more feminine wardrobes after our weeks at sea. Carlos offered plenty of bargains, since the exchange rate was fifty Argentine pesos to a single U.S. dollar. Both ladies bought dresses, sexy underwear, and leather boots. The goods were inexpensive, but finding room to stow a lot more luggage on *Dolphin* was a challenge.

Though clothes were readily available for purchase, it was almost impossible to buy certain consumer goods like toilet paper, kerosene, rice, and other staples. Everybody, tourists and locals alike, had to wait in line for basic supplies, and people were becoming restive. At that time, the Argentine economy was experiencing hyperinflation of roughly one percent per day. There was a thriving black market, and not just in basic goods. We sought out "unofficial" *cambios* (money exchangers) who gave us much better rates than the banks. But whether we offered pesos or U.S. dollars, we were unable to buy any kerosene for the next leg of our voyage and we had to hope that we did not run out along the way. There was just no kerosene available anywhere in Mar del Plata.

Some aspects of the black market appeared quite comical, at least to us as foreigners. At the train station, we saw a man dressed in a long, oversized trench coat. As commuters walked passed him, he "flashed" open his coat to reveal a few dozen toilet rolls for sale. Some people discretely bought a roll or two. Others were more desperate and shoved forward, pushing one another. A policeman blew his whistle and everyone dispersed in a hurry. I found this particularly amusing, although I expected my crew to use squares of newspaper, just as I had done when I was a kid growing up during the Depression.

Alfie was overwhelmed by the sheer size and culture of Mar del Plata—a city of several million people. He had never been out of his hometown, Punta Arenas, before sailing on *Le Dauphin*. As a fisherman, he had learned his local waters but he had never ventured further afield. His first train ride amazed him, and he was just as astonished by the fifty flavors of ice cream available in an ice cream parlor. His naïve pleasure in modern city amenities was charming.

Distinguished by her U.S. flag as the only non-Argentine boat in the marina, *Dolphin* was quite an attraction, and we found ourselves sought after as dinner guests by the social elite of Mar del Plata. It wasn't just that we were exotic foreigners. People saw us as modern day adventurers, braving the wild ocean in our small yacht. Everyone wanted to know our story.

July 1 was the first anniversary of Juan Peron's death, and the occasion for a mourning procession in downtown Mar del Plata. *Dolphin*'s entire crew were invited to dinner by a couple from the Mar del Plata yacht club, Douglas and Daisy Jenkins. Their home was a magnificent Spanish-style *hacienda,* complete with courtyard, in an exclusive neighborhood of the city. They prepared an *asado,* a local form of BBQ, for us. No amount of quality beef, *chorizo* (sausage), prawns, and salmon was too much for their honored guests. We were served fine wines, a quartet of violinists performed during dinner, and a guitarist and a woman in a bright red dress performed a Spanish flamenco song and dance. We had sweet cakes with honey for dessert and forty-year-old port to finish off. It was a marvelous evening. We got a ride back to the boat at 1 a.m., and although Réanne and I had to put in our morning appearance at the *Prefectura*, Trev, Alfie, and Margie slept in until midday.

Another yacht club couple, Clara Caeira and her lawyer husband, hosted us the next night. They took us to their opulent home up in the hills, and we ate *empanadas* with salads and French champagne. The evening was filled with lively political debate and conversation, both in English and *Castellano,* the Spanish dialect of the region. We met a Belgian diplomat, a French ambassador, and many influential Argentines. Once again, we arrived home in the early hours of the morning, and were greeted at the entrance of the yacht club by our friend Atilio, the "doorman," as I referred to him. I showed him our appreciation by giving him one of the U.S. silver dollars from my stash.

Every night we found ourselves guests of another family. We generally found the conversation and camaraderie we shared with these people both stimulating and enjoyable. One prominent family shared a story of political woe. Their father was being held by kidnappers for a multi-million dollar ransom, and they were anxiously awaiting news of any kind. Their home was by far the most opulent we visited in the region. An original Picasso oil painting hung on the wall in the entrance to their luxurious home. The kidnappers obviously knew their target.

It was a good thing our Mar del Plata social life was so captivating. Without the *zarpe*, we were under house (or boat-) arrest and unable to leave for Buenos Aires until we were given official permission to do so. It was *Dolphin*'s first safe port since Acapulco so we slept well at night, but we were essentially stuck. Réanne and I continued to make daily appearances at the *Prefectura* with no word on our *zarpe*. After more than a week of this, I decided it was time to take charge. I wouldn't pay a bribe, but I thought a bit of theater might encourage the officials. Réanne and I were seated in an alcove in one of the rooms out of the sight line of the three officers who were in charge of our case and who obviously hoped we would see reason and cough up a bribe. Knowing they were listening, I winked at Réanne and said loudly, "Boy, we were treated much better by the Chileans. These Argentinian guys could sure learn from them."

"You're right," Réanne replied, equally loudly. "They really treat foreigners pretty badly here. I think we should call the U.S. Ambassador when we get back to the boat, don't you?"

"Absolutely," I said. "We should have called the U.S. Ambassador a week ago!"

We kept this up for a couple of minutes. Next thing we knew, the officers had reappeared, all smiles, papers in hand. "*Capitán* Douglass, here is your *zarpe*. We just got the clearance from Puerto Madryn. Have a good voyage!"

Our final permission to leave was granted on July 4. It was both Independence Day back home and for *Dolphin* in Mar del Plata. I planned an immediate departure for the following morning, so we spent our last full day in Mar del Plata preparing for the 300-mile voyage northward to Buenos Aires. Groceries were delivered to the boat in the early afternoon. Réanne and Margie spent a couple of hours packing and storing canned and fresh foods away in the cupboards, while Alfie, Trev and I loaded water and diesel. We still hadn't been able to buy kerosene anywhere.

That evening, the yacht club held a farewell dinner in our honor. There were about thirty guests, many of whom had been our hosts on previous evenings. The captain of the club and his girlfriend, Ruby Gliksman, were the hosts on this particular occasion. Ruby was an interpreter and radio announcer in Mar del Plata. Margie particularly enjoyed Ruby's company and had learned that Ruby's grandfather was one of the original members of the 1855 expedition that discovered Victoria Falls in what was then Rhodesia. Ruby seemed to enjoy our company too. She gave Trev the address of one of her theater friends in Buenos Aires, which he appreciated. As a professional stage designer, Trev was quite interested in learning about Argentine theater craft.

We were seated at dinner with our friends Hector and Rachel. The meal of the evening was *paella,* a delicious dish with seafood, rice, saffron sauce, and chicken, topped with mussels and calamari, and presented at the table in clay pots. The wine was superb and the company excellent.

I made a speech to thank the yacht club members for their hospitality and commemorating American Independence Day. We were all grateful for the friends we made in Mar del Plata, and for the outstanding hospitality we had received.

Ruby spoke eloquently of our bravery on the high seas and presented us with a miniature bronze running light, mounted on a plaque with the club colors and badge engraved on it. I was quite touched and thanked everyone with genuine tears in my eyes. But the evening wasn't over yet. I quietly asked Trev, Alfie, and Margie to go on ahead to *Dolphin* and light the lamps, since I had invited several guests aboard for after dinner drinks. Of course, "several" turned out to be about a dozen, so we had seventeen people huddled in *Dolphin*'s cabin, chatting, signing the guest register, and staring around at the little boat that had come so far, all saying, "Unbelievable!" and "Amazing!"

Though the last person left at 0200 hours, Réanne and Margie were up relatively early the next morning and walked up to the *barrio* to buy a few last minute provisions. They also managed to buy a quart of kerosene by pleading with the crew of another boat, succeeding where we mere men had failed.

Our friend in the clothing business, Carlos, joined us for the sailing voyage to Buenos Aires. I took him to the *Prefectura* to complete the necessary paperwork, but this went smoothly, and Carlos brought his gear aboard *Le Dauphin*.

Atilio, the old man who had first escorted Dolphin into the harbor, came aboard and gave Margie a pretty silk scarf. She and Trev delighted him with a new megaphone which they painted and decorated for him. I gave him several silver dollars as a goodbye gift, which pleased him at least as much.

Ruby, Hector and Rachel, and Douglas Jenkins and his children all ran along the quay waving and shouting encouraging words. Some of them joined Atilio aboard his small dinghy and accompanied us to the end of the *Club Nautico* basin. We departed much as we had arrived, with Atilio shouting "Take it easy, *amigos!*" through his fancy new megaphone. We waved our farewells and sailed away from Mar del Plata with tears in our eyes.

Sailing conditions out of Mar del Plata were fantastic, with clear weather and a Force 5 wind. We hoisted all the sails and flew along at seven knots. Alfie pointed out penguins in the water—two or three at a time, then a larger group of fifteen or more. White and grey albatrosses soared alongside us. A mile from shore, we observed an unbroken line of beautiful, deserted beaches and sand dunes. Carlos said they were good places for dune buggying and camping in the summer.

The wind picked up by evening, and the sea began to get choppy. As the leeward rail disappeared below the water surface, we dropped the mainsail. Another *pampero*? Maybe. It was certainly more than a squall. Réanne, Carlos and Margie were all throwing up. The girls kept to their bunks but Carlos preferred to stay on deck. By midnight the wind had all but died away, though the seas remained bouncy. I started the engine and saw bioluminescence in our wake for the first time since the Pacific. There were lights along the coast, and when Alfie came on watch

I reminded him not to steer toward them, but to sail according to the compass and keep us on a heading parallel to the coast.

Dolphin heeling to the strong winds of the South Atlantic

As the sun rose, so did the wind. Conditions were similar to the previous day. The log book read "Winds NW F6-7. Much spray and strain. Very bad chop—boat thrown on beam ends. Silverware drawer falls out." The crew were still sick and even I was beginning to feel under the weather. Sailing northward meant having to fight against both wind and current, with little progress to show for it. I gave up and set a course into shore where the seas were calmer. The water was a peculiar chocolate color and surprisingly shallow. Fifty yards off shore, in fourteen feet of water, I gave the order to drop anchor.

Rather than fighting the adverse north wind, *Dolphin* remained at anchor for another day and night. The crew caught up on sleep and meals missed due to seasickness. Sitting at anchor wasn't going to get us the remaining 250 miles to Buenos Aires, however. The next morning we took advantage of a favorable wind, hoisted the sails, and headed back out to sea. The water remained muddy brown and weirdly shallow. Even out of sight of land, the depth sounder showed only twenty feet.

Darkness came early in the Southern Hemisphere's winter, but it brought the stars with it, reflected in an ocean that was now still as a pond. Venus and a bright moon cast their light across the water. The Milky Way aligned almost perfectly north to south. Trev found an oval cluster of stars shaped just like an Easter egg directly overhead. I brought out my sextant for star sights, but set our course primarily by sightings on the lighthouses along the coast.

At 1830 hours, Punta Piedras light was dead ahead, bearing 305 degrees. At 0120 hours, the bearing had shifted to 175 degrees. We were right on course.

As the day dawned, a heavy mist set in and visibility was poor. I looked for the Punta Alaya light but couldn't see it. The others took bets on where Buenos Aires actually was, but I had more faith in my navigation than they did. We passed a series of large, anchored ships and then a line of electrical pylons, confirming our position. Finally, late in the morning of July 9, the city itself came into view. But now something else made me nervous. I switched on the AM radio and was alarmed to hear the Argentine national anthem playing on all stations, followed by the Hallelujah Chorus. One of the people we had met along the way had warned us that if we heard broadcasts of funeral music, it meant a revolution was underway. I thought seriously for a few minutes about skipping Buenos Aires and heading straight for Uruguay, but Réanne figured out we were actually listening to an Argentine Independence Day program from the National Cathedral. We continued into Buenos Aires as planned and tied up at 1550 hours at the plush Yacht Club of Argentina in the heart of the Buenos Aires waterfront. Our relief at arriving was short-lived, since the city was the center of an undeclared civil war.

Chapter 5

Buenos Aires, Argentina

9 July - 19 November, 1975

Buenos Aires is one of the world's great cities. A major metropolis, it is the capital city of Argentina and known as the "Paris of South America" for its elegant European-style architecture, multicultural population, and rich cultural life. During our visit in 1975, it was also a city out of control. An undeclared civil war known as the Dirty War raged between the right-wing government of Isabel Peron and several left-wing revolutionary groups. Prominent citizens were being assassinated, and ordinary people simply disappeared. Similar political unrest was starting to happen in Chile, too, but we had been fortunate to receive exceptional personal treatment from the Chilean Navy in Punta Arenas. Perhaps Pinochet's philosophy and methods had not yet taken root in the remotest part of Chile, and we were the beneficiaries of the professionalism and culture that predated his coup. By contrast, I found Buenos Aires to be outrageously corrupt and dangerous. *Dolphin* spent the next four months there, and to this day I consider it a miracle that we all got away from the city unscathed, *Dolphin* included. The boat of a prominent politician was blown up in our marina during our stay. It had been moored only a few slips away, and the debris rained down on our decks.

We had little understanding of the politics and intended to stay in Buenos Aires only until Dolphin's repairs were complete. None of us became casualties of the Dirty War, though we were to have plenty of close calls. I was also fortunate to escape the fate of Hal Roth. After repairing his damaged yacht, *Whisper*, in Buenos Aires, he had then been arrested and forced to pay a fine for arguing with the Argentine authorities. Roth departed Buenos Aires only two weeks before our arrival, leaving *Dolphin* one of only two American sailboats in the entire city. I worried that we would be seen as a target ripe for exploitation by either side.

After a few days at the downtown Yacht Club of Argentina, we relocated *Dolphin* to the San Fernando Yacht Club about thirty miles north of Buenos Aires, in Tigre. San Fernando was home to José Parodi's boatyard. Parodi specialized in building wooden yachts, and had the experience to tackle our lengthy repair list. After a brisk day sail to Tigre, we tied up next to a gorgeous wooden ketch called *Gaucho*. She was designed by the renowned marine architect Manuel Campos and was built at Parodi's boatyard. Her first owner, a famous Argentine sailor named Ernesto Uriburu, sailed her around the Atlantic for two years in the 1950s and wrote several classic books about his voyages. In 1975, *Gaucho* was owned by an American, Tony Badger. As we got to know Tony, we told him about *Dolphin*'s adventures. Tony told both Margie and me that he'd set out from the U.S. with his wife and two young daughters aboard, but his wife had disappeared during the voyage south. Tony didn't say exactly what had happened to her, but I later found out she had actually died of cancer in California before their trip. I never learned why he misled us about the facts of her death.

Tony was writing an article about Manuel Campos for a sailing magazine and met with him frequently. Campos was interested in hearing about our pitchpole experience, so Tony introduced us to him. Réanne and I were both so excited to meet Campos that we could hardly sit still during his visit. He commented that *Dolphin* must be extremely well built, which accounted for our survival. He invited me to give him a phone call when Parodi hauled *Dolphin* out for hull repairs, and he offered to survey her damages without charge.

Campos's career spanned sixty-four years and he produced more than 200 designs for strong, safe, and seaworthy boats. He was a modest man, not a self-promoter, and he was a pioneer of cruising yacht design. One of his most famous boats, *LEGH II*, was built for the famous Argentine yachtsman Vito Dumas who sailed single-handed around the three great capes of the Southern Hemisphere in the 1940's. Even in his 80's, Campos was still active in the boatyard, regularly visiting to oversee the restoration of *LEGH II* for eventual display at the Naval Museum of Argentina. His designs all emphasized seaworthiness and comfort over speed, arguing that, "You can't eat your soup at more than twenty degrees of heel." It was a great honor to have him assess *Dolphin* and advise on her repairs.

One morning shortly after our arrival, a young man came over to our slip and introduced himself. Victor was dressed in grimy work clothes when we met, but he turned out to be an attorney with excellent connections in Buenos Aires society. His father had been a friend of the aforementioned Ernesto Uriburu, and Victor himself owned a yacht at the marina called *Joanne*. Victor kept his politics close to his chest and he knew how to get things done within Argentina's corruption. During our stay, he proved to be a useful acquaintance, helping us overcome bureaucratic obstacles and introducing me to some extremely interesting people. He asked a lot of questions about visa problems and finding work in America, and Réanne and I quickly realized that he saw us as a possible ticket out of Argentina. In return for his help, I agreed to sign him up as crew.

The danger, discomfort, and expense of *Dolphin*'s voyage so far, as well as the distance from her family, all strengthened Réanne's resolve to return to California. She found her decision easier once she knew she wasn't leaving me to continue alone. Trev, Margie, and Alfie had all stepped up during our challenging voyage to Buenos Aires. Although not expert mariners, all three were capable people, with the willingness to learn and the spirit of adventure it would take to sail across the Atlantic. Victor was an experienced sailor, and he would make a good addition to the crew. After repairs, I now planned to take *Dolphin* across the South Atlantic from Argentina to Cape Town, South Africa. Margie and Trev were South African citizens and they spoke positively about the relative lack of corruption and bombings there. I suggested to Réanne that she might rejoin *Dolphin* in South Africa to continue our circumnavigation.

Réanne's departure from Buenos Aires came sooner rather than later, since she figured she could fit in a quick visit to friends in France on her way home to California. Booking a flight to Paris was easy enough. The more difficult part was changing the Argentine entry stamp in her passport from "crew member entitled to leave country only by boat" to a regular tourist visa. This required a visit to the immigration office downtown and standing in a line several blocks long. At this point, our new friend Victor proved his usefulness as he greased a palm or two and took us straight into the building where a senior official resolved her visa problem in a matter of minutes. Réanne was doubly grateful for Victor's assistance. Otherwise she would have been faced with the prospect of trying to explain what she needed to a *petit bureaucrat* who failed to understand her Spanish. It amused her that educated Spanish-speakers understood her well enough; it was always the minor officials who had the problems.

On the day she was due to fly out, Réanne and I caught the train from San Fernando into Buenos Aires to do some shopping. A general work stoppage had been called later in the day for some kind of political protest. The shops were still open when we arrived downtown and we were able to complete most of our errands by mid-morning. We then walked through some of the galleries on Florida Avenue, the mile-long, pedestrian-only thoroughfare that runs through the heart of the city. I saw a wooden carving of a gaucho that I liked, and we were in the process of bargaining over the price when we heard a loud group of protesters approaching. The proprietor of our shop immediately rolled down a metal security gate out front, turned off the lights inside, and locked the doors. Réanne and I stood quietly inside with him as the agitators passed by outside shouting *"¡Cerra!"* ("Close!"), pounding on each door or gate as they made their way down the street. This same experience happened to us twice more that morning, and by noon almost all of the downtown stores were closed and shuttered. The proprietors made it clear that they disagreed with the protestors. I was able to buy the gaucho carving and I still have it.

Réanne flew out later that evening. She had too much luggage with her, which prompted only a Gallic shrug from the Air France crew but caused a variety of problems with the Argentine airport officials. Réanne was relieved to leave Argentina for somewhere more civilized. Because of strikes, her flight to Paris was the only one leaving Buenos Aires that night, and all incoming flights were being diverted just across the River Platte to Montevideo, Uruguay. Réanne wrote from France a few days later that it was "a strange sensation taking off down the runway of an airport which serves eleven million people and knowing that ours was the only plane to do so."

I saw another sample of life under Argentina's military dictatorship as Victor drove me back from the airport to San Fernando. The road was a broad multi-lane highway, but we were forced into the slow lane by a convoy of official vehicles speeding past us with lights flashing and sirens blaring. All the other private cars on the road were moving over too, but as the last of the government vehicles, a pickup truck full of soldiers, drove past us, a braided hat belonging to an officer in the truck flew off and rolled in front of us. The hat's owner jumped out and ran back against the traffic, pistol in hand, to retrieve it. Victor swerved to miss it and the cars behind us all swerved too. I really thought that if someone had driven over that hat, the officer would have shot him.

After Réanne's departure, work on *Dolphin*'s repairs began in earnest at the Parodi boatyard. Manual laborers performed all of the work, including hauling boats out of the water. A donkey engine winch dragged the boats up from the water on wooden skids, with men on each side spreading grease to ease the way. The skids used to pull *Dolphin* up from the water were too narrow, and she settled too quickly onto the supports, breaking one of her ribs and puncturing her hull in two places. The workmen repaired the broken rib with a stout "sister" rib and replanked the punctures. The original repair list was already long and involved, including the broken spreaders at the top of the mast, and the work progressed very slowly. I got frustrated with the two-steps-forward, one-step-back progress. I tried to coax the workmen along, but they were not paid very much and had no particular reason to work carefully or to hurry and finish the job. I didn't want to spend any more time in Buenos Aires than I had to, so I had to figure out a way to motivate the boatyard workers to put in a little more effort. Each morning before they started work, the men sat around drinking *mate*. This is a caffeinated tea-like beverage brewed from the dried leaves of the *yerba* bush, a South American holly-like plant, and it is the unofficial national drink of Argentina. Because of the economic situation in the country at that time, most people, including the boatyard workers, had to drink their *mate* without sugar, which made it much less palatable. Sugar was rationed in Argentina, but *Dolphin* had a ten-pound bag in her stores, so I gave it to the boatyard workers. After that, they greeted me with enthusiasm whenever they saw me, and repair work on the boat proceeded much more briskly. I'm proud that I've never directly bribed anyone, but a little grease—or sugar—certainly helped get the wheels turning.

Of course, the boatyard workers expected more from me than sugar. When I arrived in Buenos Aires, I didn't have any money, but I had received a telegram from my business partner in California confirming that a $30,000 insurance check had been forwarded to me in care of the Port Captain. Buenos Aires is as big as New York City, and the Port Captain's office was located in a large building downtown. When I went in, everybody was watching a soccer game on TV.

"I'm Don Douglass and I'm expecting a letter from California," I said.

No one was interested in helping me. Nobody would even talk to me. If my check had ever arrived at the Port Captain's office, it was long gone. Luckily, one of Réanne's former Pomona College roommates was from an upper class Argentine family. She had told us before we left on our round-the-world sailing trip that we should contact her if we needed any assistance while we were in Argentina. She was back in California when we arrived in Buenos Aires, but I got in touch with her father and the first thing he did was invite me to a party. I put on my most respectable clothes, a clean shirt and sports coat, and turned up at the address I'd been given. This turned out to be a nondescript multi-story building with a bank of elevators, but no directory to tell me which floor I wanted. I was standing there at a loss, when a formally dressed couple walked up to me and asked if I needed help.

"Well," I said, "I was invited to a party here, but I only have the street address, not the apartment number or floor."

"Welcome, *Señor*," the gentleman replied courteously. "That apartment is served by a private elevator. Please allow me to assist you."

The couple escorted me to one of the elevators and keyed in a security code. The elevator rose and opened directly into an elegant foyer, where I was graciously welcomed into a crowd that included admirals, generals, bodyguards and the like, not to mention some of the most stunning women I have ever seen in my life. One man with an impressive amount of gold braid on his uniform soaked up the compliments I made about his country, "Beautiful women, wonderful beef, the most refined wines ..."

In return, he said to me, "You are very gracious, *Señor*. Is there anything we can do for you while you are here?"

"I've lost a check," I said. "It was sent in care of the Port Captain, and I know it arrived because my bank manager sent me a confirmation note."

General 'X' called over one of his aides. "*Capitán* Douglass has a problem with the Port Captain. Look into this for him."

I didn't really expect anything to come of the conversation, but I remember leaving the party thinking, "Well, at least I tried." In the meantime, I had cultivated the friendship of the security guard who manned the entrance gate to the yacht club. He kept an eye on everyone who came and went, and he also answered all of the incoming phone calls. One day he beckoned me over and said, "*Capitán*, General 'X' has called and asks that you return his phone call." I was a bit dismissive but the guard was insistent: "*Capitán*, General 'X' is an important man. I think you should call him now." I called the number I was given and was told to call the Port Captain again. So I called the Port Captain and he said, "If you go to the Central Bank of Argentina and ask for Teller Number 52, you will receive your money." I figured a bit of flattery was in order. "You really take care of us sailors," I said, or something like that, trying not to sound too facetious.

A short time later a beautiful woman in a Mercedes came to collect me from the yacht club. The car had a license plate indicating she was among the city's elite, able to drive—and park—anywhere she wanted. She took me to the Central Bank where I asked for Teller Number 52, who duly produced the check. It had been endorsed with my name, but the money had clearly been paid to someone else. When I pointed this out, the teller waved a dismissive hand. "No matter, *Señor*. How would you like your money?"

In the midst of all the violence and political upheaval, the Argentine economy took a nosedive. Inflation was as high as eighty percent in 1975, and consumer prices doubled between May and August alone. This had very practical consequences for me. I asked to have my insurance check paid to me in U.S. dollars so I could convert it to Argentine pesos a little at a time. Due to the rampant inflation, both the official and the unofficial or black market exchange rates changed daily, so I didn't want to exchange dollars for pesos until the day I really needed them. I had to exchange money several times a week because the Argentine contractors who were working on my boat would only accept cash. A woman at the U.S. Embassy told me that I could get three times the money if I went to an unofficial exchanger instead of a bank. In fact, she told me to go to the Thomas Cook travel agency next to the main Buenos Aires police station and ask at the front counter for "Maria." I followed these instructions, and was directed to one of the tellers, who accepted my cash and gave me a piece of paper in return. There were no names on it, just the number of dollars I had handed over for exchange. She then sent me downstairs to a man sitting behind a one-way glass window.

"Maria sent me," I said. The man took the paper, gave me back a wad of pesos that turned out, sure enough, to be three times the posted rate. "Maria" was a different person every time I went there. One day I was directed to a supervisor, a big guy with three guns on him, counting out thousands of bills. I decided not to change money that day. On another occasion, "Maria" said to me, "I can't help you today." She leaned forward and whispered quickly, "The police are inspecting at one o'clock. Please leave now." So there I was, part of the same corrupt system, but what else could I do?

Before I get too self-righteous, I should confess that Réanne and I engaged in a little conspiracy of our own. The U.S. government only allowed its citizens to take a maximum of $10,000 out of the country at any one time, and I needed quite a bit more than the insurance money to cover the boat repairs and my expenses in Buenos Aires. During my stay there, I had to fly back home to Southern California a couple of times to check up on my WGI business. The company was marking time in my absence, but I wasn't satisfied with the direction my temporary chief was taking things. I used the return trips as an opportunity to bring more money back to Argentina. Réanne, in the meantime, knitted me some heavy socks with double soles. When I flew back to Buenos Aires, I would declare to US Customs that I was taking no more than $10,000 with me—omitting to mention the additional $5,000 hidden in each of my socks.

The black market in Argentina extended to all sorts of commodities, not just money. The entire economy was controlled by monopolies, which set their own, generally exorbitant, prices, so there were always people offering you stuff on the cheap. Just as I had seen in Mar del Plata, some commodities were almost impossible to obtain. I needed several hundred gallons of diesel for the next leg of my voyage, but I could buy only five gallons at a time. Every day Alfie filled a five-gallon can at the service station near the marina and carried it back to *Dolphin*. My friend Victor was visiting one day, and told me he could "take care of it." He arranged for a gas truck to run a hose directly to our boat and fill up our fuel tanks, saving Alfie the trouble of doing it the hard way. Victor certainly knew the right way to get things done. He also helped me when I realized I had almost outstayed my Argentine visa, which would have meant big trouble with the immigration authorities. Victor took me to the guard at the building entrance and explained that I was an American who would be leaving Argentina in a few days, so I needed to get my papers taken care of as soon as possible. An Argentine banknote worth something like twenty dollars slipped between Victor and the guard, although the transaction was done by sleight of hand so that no one actually saw it. Suddenly I was at the head of the long line. Adding a little sweetener was certainly the most efficient way to get things accomplished in Buenos Aires.

After Réanne's departure, I was a single man in a big city, and Victor helped me find ways to enjoy myself. Before Réanne left, we agreed to have an open marriage for as long as I continued sailing without her. To me, an open marriage meant just that. I didn't want there to be any secrets between us, so I wrote her when Victor fixed me up with someone to translate and provide other services. Magela was a woman of a certain age, a former B-movie actress, who knew her way around Buenos Aires. She was helpful in a practical sense, and she was also happy to take care of me in other, more personal ways. Although no longer young, Magela was good looking and she was very careful with her appearance, always attractively dressed and heavily made up. One day, Victor took us to an old *hacienda* with a swimming pool. I splashed Magela playfully. All her makeup ran down her face, and she looked like a melting wax model. It was one of the funniest things I had ever seen, and I roared with laughter, although she was not a bit amused.

Victor also showed me some of the Buenos Aires nightlife. At that time, the city was home to several really fancy nightclubs—the sort of place where the women were almost all six foot tall models wearing nothing but a few strategically placed feathers. On one occasion Victor asked if I'd like to see the "inner show." Of course! We were admitted to an inner room, occupied by a circle of men seated on chairs so close together that their knees were almost touching. The inner circle was only four or five feet across, but the room was so dark you couldn't see anything. Victor and I joined them, and then a spotlight came on and a beautiful naked woman came out to dance seductively in the middle of the circle, barely a foot or two in front of us. What a turn on!

Victor arranged access to a luxury apartment in the heart of the city. It was a full-service establishment, almost like a hotel suite in an outwardly nondescript old brownstone building. The apartment could be reserved for anything from a couple of hours to days or more, and room service was available if needed. The building's apartments were obviously used by the city's elite for discreet assignations, and I stayed there with Magela while my crew watched over *Dolphin* in the San Fernando boatyard. I also used it as a safe-house during periods of civil unrest. Several times, both Victor and the friendly guard at the yacht club gate gave me advance warning of "rumbles" or other disturbances. My concern was not so much for myself, or for my male crewmembers, but for Margie and Magela. Once or twice Margie spent a night in the apartment while Trev, Alfie and I kept watch on *Dolphin*, shining a spotlight on the U.S. flag that I'd hung in the rigging.

In addition to Magela, I befriended several other women in Buenos Aires. One night, after an evening of fun with Victor, I brought a young lady back to *Dolphin* one evening to show her around. We were just getting comfortable when Margie returned from a late dinner, and I was surprised at her possessive attitude.

"Don, I live here," she yelled at me. "You can't just bring some woman off the streets into my home for your entertainment! Get a room!" I didn't know what Margie was so upset about, since she and Trev had the aft bunks for their own private time, but I escorted my acquaintance elsewhere just to keep the peace.

The longer we stayed in Buenos Aires, the more we found ourselves caught up in the undeclared revolution. I got tired of people pointing guns at me with their fingers on the triggers. One afternoon, while I was walking down one of the wide streets, a truck full of partisans roared past me. They were tossing out bundles of propaganda leaflets. One big bale just missed me. It would have killed me if it had connected, and it didn't matter to me in the least which side had thrown it.

At least one attempted coup occurred during our stay. It was carried out by a small group of lower-ranking Air Force officers who were not supported by the men in command. The activists flew over the Casa Rosada (the Buenos Aires White House) and sprayed it with bullets. The building looked fine when I passed by one afternoon, but the next day it was pockmarked with bullet holes. The higher-ups apparently took the view that if you wanted to avoid being shot, you remained loyal until the time was right—at which time you were no longer loyal. I had the sense that the countdown to open revolution was getting short, and was foolish enough to declare at a party one night that I knew the exact date the revolution would occur. People looked at me quizzically and asked "When? How could an American know this?" I explained that I'd walked all over Buenos Aires by this time and had noticed that all of the major streets were named after the dates of past Argentine revolutions. As far as I could tell, the only date not taken was July 5th. The crowd laughed nervously, and I realized I should have kept my mouth shut. Being American conferred a sort of privilege, but if the wrong people had been there and taken offense, I would have been in trouble.

Argentine society was extremely stratified, with a small middle class and little contact between the rich and the poor. Trev, Margie, Alfie and I all had quite different experiences of the city. I mingled with the elite and was invited to expensive bars and some wild parties where I met actresses and political power brokers. I had never mixed in such high society before. Dinner parties were segregated by sex; the trophy wives sat together and chatted about haute couture, exotic vacations, and plastic surgery, while the men discussed political maneuvering and financial markets. Trev and Margie didn't meet the social elites, but they went to mid-level restaurants and met a variety of students and activists with hair-curling political views. Their friends steered them to even better black-market exchange rates.

Alfie learned a little about the city's lowlife. As we got ready to depart, we all usually slept aboard the boat, but one night Alfie didn't return. I had no idea how to go about finding him if he got into trouble, but fortunately he reappeared the following morning. He was out of breath and insisted on remaining below deck. Bit by bit, I got the story out of him. He had a bit of cash and decided to spend it on getting laid. Someone in the city directed him to a large whorehouse where clients were offered drinks and appetizers while the women of the house paraded before them. Alfie assumed the refreshments were free, but he got cold feet when the time came for him to choose a companion, at which point the manager presented him with the bill. It was a lot more money than Alfie was carrying, so he did the only thing he could think of—he ran. Thugs from the whorehouse chased after him, but the yacht club was several miles out of town and Alfie managed to lose them. He made it back safely, and after that he stayed aboard every night until we sailed.

After *Dolphin*'s repairs were complete and just before we were due to leave, an army truck stopped on the road into the yacht club, as close as it could get to our boat. There was a grassy patch between the road and the water, and a line of regularly spaced trees. A half-dozen soldiers jumped out of the back of the truck and positioned themselves behind the trees, with the guns all aimed at me, their fingers on the triggers. In spite of how scary it was, I thought it funny that the soldiers were all wearing tennis shoes with their army uniforms. Then an officer got out of the truck, .45 pistol in hand, and came part way across the grass toward me.

"*Capitán* Douglass?" he shouted.

"That's me," I shouted back. I was standing on the dock, but I grabbed the rail of the boat with my hand. According to maritime law, *Dolphin* was U.S. territory. As long as I was in contact with her I was not technically in Argentina but in transit.

"I need to talk to you," the officer said.

"I can hear you from here," I replied, not letting go of the rail.

The officer was stymied. "You are *Capitán* Douglass?" he said again.

"Yes, just like I said."

Meanwhile, Trev did some quick thinking. He grabbed *Dolphin*'s radio microphone and shouted into it loudly enough for the officer to hear, "This is the United States yacht *Dolphin*. Patch me through to the U.S. Embassy. Repeat, U.S. Embassy."

The officer stepped back to consider the situation. "Very well," he said. He turned and went back to his truck. His men lowered their guns and followed him, and they drove away. I think the officer decided that arresting me was a decision above his pay grade. He had confirmed my identity, and that was the end of the matter. I'm a stubborn guy and this was one occasion when standing my ground was the right thing to have done.

After four months in Buenos Aires, I was extremely relieved when *Dolphin*'s repairs were finally finished. Even with Magela's translating and Victor's bribes, trying to get the complex job done in the midst of warring political factions, hyper-inflation, and general corruption had been a nerve-wracking experience. The workmen had done a fine job relatively cheaply, since U.S. dollars went a long way in the Argentine economy. As we got ready to depart, Victor and I filled out the paperwork so he could sail with us as one of *Dolphin*'s crew, and he brought aboard a duffle with some clothing. I was looking forward to having another experienced sailor on board to share the work of crossing the South Atlantic to Cape Town.

I decided to throw a big party at the yacht club to thank all of the people who had helped us, and to say goodbye to all the friends we had made. Long, rough-sawn planks set up on saw horses acted as our tables. We had three kinds of grilled meats served directly onto the wood, along with rich Argentine Malbec. Plates were regarded as unnecessary, and the people jabbed their steak knives and forks right into the cedar planks. I thought this was a waste of the fine wood, but it seemed quite usual to everyone there. I hired two local street musicians to entertain the guests. They were young men who played fantastic guitar duets on a single beat-up instrument. They played so well that before we set sail the next morning, I took them to a music shop and bought them a second guitar. It cost me almost nothing, but they could never have afforded it themselves. They were two delighted kids. Victor never showed up at the party, or at the boat the next day, and in fact I never heard from him again. At the party, Tony gave Margie a bit of a warning about Victor's amorous reputation, telling her to watch out if he did indeed sail with us, so she was relieved when he didn't show up. Victor had only wanted papers for entry to the U.S. as part of *Dolphin*'s crew. I thought it was damn deceitful of him at the time, but he also made my time in Buenos Aires a lot easier and more pleasant, so overall, it was a pretty fair bargain.

Alfie filling water jugs before departure

Chapter 6

Buenos Aires, Argentina to Tristan da Cunha

19 November 1975 - 9 December 1975

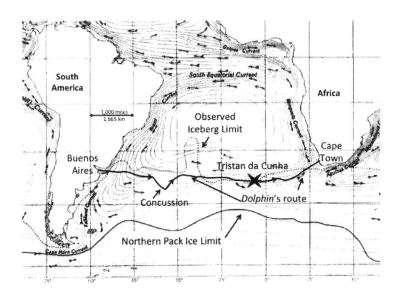

I was eager to leave Buenos Aires and sail *Dolphin* across the South Atlantic from Argentina to Cape Town, South Africa. My planned trip had been delayed by *Dolphin*'s repairs, but I could still sail around the world, even without Réanne. The congenial crew eased the labor of passage-making, and I still hoped Réanne might rejoin us as we traveled onward.

On our last night in Buenos Aires, we experienced a total lunar eclipse. I persuaded the crew that it was a good omen for our successful voyage. We left Buenos Aires and Argentina around noon the next day for the trip north to Montevideo, Uruguay. Our many friends wished us farewell from the San Fernando Yacht Club, and *Dolphin* put on a fine display as we sailed out of the harbor. The crew indulged in a rousing chorus of the Jim Croce song, *New York's Not My Home*, replacing the original lyrics with disrespectful local references.

While raising the sails, Alfie let go of the main halyard and it ran right up to the top of the mast. I yelled at him that the guy who lost it had to retrieve it. Alfie was so embarrassed that he started shinnying up the mast. The boat was rocking like crazy, so I yelled at him some more: "No, stop, get down before you kill yourself!" But he kept going and recaptured the halyard. After this, we moved off in fine style—and then almost immediately ran aground on a soft sandbar. By good luck, we were out of sight of the spectators by then, and *Dolphin* was quickly refloated by the tide. Clearly we were not the only bumblers in that patch of water, since most of the channel marker buoys had been dented and bent in collisions with other ships troubled by the strong counter-currents in the river.

During the night, the southeast wind piped up, encouraging Alfie to raise all the sails. When I came on deck, we were doing a spanking eight knots, with no preventers rigged! *Dolphin* was performing well, but there was a huge risk of damage if we gybed. We sailed 200 miles in thirty-six hours and arrived in Punta del Este, Uruguay four hours ahead of our anticipated arrival time. We still had to wait offshore until dawn to enter the port, so *Dolphin*'s impressive burst of speed hadn't really saved us any time.

I planned a short stop in Punta del Este to top up fuel and water just before the long Atlantic crossing. The authorities who came aboard were extremely rude, even stubbing their cigarettes on the deck! An efficient petty officer quickly filled out the Uruguayan immigration forms, which was encouraging. Then, at 8:30 a.m., a good looking, well dressed officer arrived to tell me that the port was closed due to too much wind; that our boat might need an inspection; that I might have some trouble with my camera when ashore; and a lot of other bothersome things. He wouldn't tell me when the port would re-open. He got a little sheepish when I told him that this very boat had come from California and Easter Island via the Magellan Strait, and that she could take the conditions outside his harbor.

I stepped back into the port office after we completed the task of taking on fuel and water. Two uniformed officials told me the port was still closed. They apparently had trouble believing we had just stopped in for a few supplies. For the second time that morning I described the conditions we had already been through, and the seaworthiness of *Dolphin*. A third officer arrived. Pointing to the red storm flag flying over the port, he told me that we couldn't leave until the green flag was up. I told them that we had sailed into his port that morning with no difficulty, and that this southwest wind of Force 3-4 was the very best wind to get us to South Africa. It might be dangerous for small boats, but my boat was very strong. It was my own risk, and we would undoubtedly see worse conditions in the Atlantic. Finally, they all gave in, and we got our exit permit.

A crowd watched us depart. I thought they had come out to see if the military officials would allow a small foreign boat to violate the port closure. Alfie had changed the genoa for the twin jib, so as we rounded the breakwater and headed upwind, I called for the jib to be raised for a good driving display of seamanship. Then I saw that Alfie had put the twin jib on upside down. Regardless, it pulled strongly as I tightened the sheets, and we sailed out on four tacks, waving to all. I am sure the *Prefectura* felt justified in letting such good sailors leave the closed port, while the two or three yachtsmen on the quay probably thought we had some new kind of high-lift cruising spinnaker. At 1230 on November 21 we rounded Punte del Este. South America was now behind us. Look out, Africa! Here we come!

*   *   *   *   *

Crossing the Atlantic from west to east was not simply a matter of pointing *Dolphin*'s bow toward South Africa and Cape Town. One of the books in our shipboard reference library, a blue-bound volume called *Ocean Passages of the World*, noted that planning the best track for an individual voyage requires "skilled evaluation of all the factors controlling the voyage and modification of the shortest route accordingly." But even figuring out the "shortest route" was less than straightforward. The distance from Buenos Aires to Cape Town is more than 3,600 miles, and the earth's curvature means that a Great Circle route—a sweeping arc with a southerly dip—is shorter than sailing the rhumb line. A rhumb line is the shortest line connecting two points on a map drawn in the Mercator projection. It appears as a straight line cutting across all the longitudinal meridians at a constant angle, but it is not an accurate representation of the most efficient course on a spherical globe.

Ocean Passages recommended generally that sailing vessels traveling from Buenos Aires or Montevideo "pick up the parallel of 40°S at 30°W. Thence, keep along that parallel as far as the meridian of Greenwich, whence steer directly for Cape Town." A chart included with the book showed this trajectory as a gentle curve passing just south of Gough Island, the most southerly of the islands in the Tristan da Cunha group. Modifying factors could include seasonal weather patterns, currents, and so forth. I studied charts of South Atlantic wind and wave patterns, and concluded that since we would be sailing the route during the austral summer, we could expect decent conditions, with westerly winds to drive us most of the way. Of course, encountering much rougher winds and seas is always a risk on any ocean crossing.

A greater priority for me than sailing the shortest route was keeping my boat and crew safe from foreseeable hazards. This meant avoiding the shipping lanes and not sailing into icebergs. Though both Buenos Aires and Cape Town have pleasantly balmy climates, wayward icebergs had occasionally been sighted in the South Atlantic north of the 40th parallel. At that latitude, the warm eastward flowing South Atlantic Current intersects the cold Antarctic Circumpolar Current. A map in *Ocean Passages* depicted the "extreme limit of iceberg sightings" as a line of triangles with a significant northerly excursion between the coast of Brazil and the Tristan da Cunha island group (see map at start of chapter). *Dolphin's* proposed route crossed this boundary, so encountering an iceberg was certainly a possibility. Icebergs are huge, solid floating objects. Everyone knows what happened when the *Titanic* struck an iceberg in 1912. *Dolphin* was only a little sailboat made of cedar planks. We wouldn't stand a chance if we hit an iceberg while sailing along at five knots or more.

I was just as anxious to avoid other vessels. Our planned route stayed well north of the 40th parallel, which would keep us several hundred miles away from the main shipping lanes between Buenos Aires and Cape Town. Not only would this path allow us to stay clear of most commercial vessel traffic, we could also make a stop at the remote volcanic island of Tristan da Cunha to obtain fuel and water if needed.

As it happened, we almost collided with another boat the first night after we left Punta del Este. The other vessel was a compact little steamer, headed south—and we were sailing directly toward it! We had all our sails up and our preventer lines were tied tightly, meaning it would take a lot of work for us to change course. However, according to the maritime Rules of the Road, our sails gave us the right of way over an engine-driven

ship in the open ocean, and it was up to the steamer to change
course for us. I got on the radio to remind the steamer crew of
this, but no one answered my call. Nor was there any sign that
the vessel was changing course, so I set my crew to work untying
all the sheets and preventers while I started the engine. We
veered away just in time—they came within 200 yards of us. I
was quite upset. I got out my thousand watt spotlight, and shined
it through the windows of the bridge of the steamer as we sailed
past. No one was in the bridge house! I could only figure that the
steamer captain had made the trip numerous times before and
had never encountered any other traffic in that patch of ocean, so
he was running his ship on autopilot. But he damn near sank us,
giving me another reason to be glad that our planned route was
north of the major shipping lanes—and we saw no further
vessels until we reached Cape Town.

*   *   *   *   *

We flew along at hull speed on our first day offshore. Spray
glittered around us, and the rail dipped under the waves. We
made twelve miles in two hours. Optimism for a quick passage
ran high, but it was soon dashed as we spent the next few days
flopping around in windless calm. *Dolphin*'s heavy canvas sails
drooped limply from the masts, occasionally tightening as they
felt the changeable breeze that picked up around sunset but
failed soon after dark. We had sunny days but saw only light and
variable winds, and we could only average about three knots,
even with the engine running. We were as becalmed as if we

were in the doldrums, rolling in the big southwest swells. The placid conditions at least gave Margie and me a chance to cool off by swimming. *Dolphin* trailed a couple of safety lines for us to cling to, and Trev kept a look out for sharks, holding my .22 rifle at the ready. We teased Alfie to join us, but he just laughed and said "No, no." While in the water, I also made cursory inspections of the hull.

Dolphin ghosting along in light air

These feeble and variable winds were characteristic of the so-called horse latitudes where we were sailing. The horse latitudes are zones of calm between the equatorial trade winds and the predominantly westerly winds of the higher latitudes found in both the northern and southern hemispheres. The name is said to come from an old British sailing ship tradition. Sailors were generally paid a month's wages in advance when they signed on to a ship. The first month of a crew's work went to pay off their advance wages, so the men didn't start earning additional pay until a month into the voyage. This first month of the trip was called "the horse," and the expression "beating a dead horse" meant trying to get extra work out of a crew while they were still working off their advance wages. Some crews held a ceremony to celebrate the date when they'd worked off their advances, and they would throw an effigy of a horse overboard. In the days of sailing ships, it took most vessels out of England a month or more to reach the latitudes in which we were sailing.

Now that we had finally left land behind, I began to take closer stock of my crew, Alfie, Trev, and Margie. We had lived and worked together in close quarters during our rough trip from Punta Arenas to Buenos Aires, and during *Dolphin's* four and a half months in the shipyard. This passage across a relatively untraveled part of the South Atlantic would shape them from inexperienced sailors into a reliable blue-water crew. I knew them as individuals who lacked sailing experience, but during our voyage so far, I had observed that they were reliable and teachable. My expectations were more than fulfilled, as they each showed tremendous initiative when called upon, readily learning from experience. Just as important, we all worked well together.

Everyone had arrived on the vessel with different skills and expectations. I spent some time in the early days thoroughly reviewing basic seamanship and everyone's duties under all possible weather conditions or emergencies. As Captain, my responsibility was for the safety of my crew and ship, and I was also legally responsible for the crew's entry and exit from the countries we would visit. We had thorough discussions of the working and living conditions on board. We had to be totally self-sufficient, and our supplies were limited. *Dolphin* carried only 120 gallons of fresh water in her two tanks. I estimated that the South Atlantic crossing from Buenos Aires to Tristan da Cunha would take twenty to thirty days. For safety, I limited fresh water consumption to two quarts per person per day, leaving us an ample reserve in case of delay. I didn't want to share the fate of Coleridge's Ancient Mariner: "Water, water everywhere, nor any drop to drink." We did our laundry in seawater, which left clothing unpleasantly sticky and damp, as the salt never quite dried. Margie even used seawater in some of the food preparation, for example in cooking porridge or rice. We also had a limited amount of kerosene for the stove and *Dolphin's* kerosene running lights.

I emphasized that we had to keep *Dolphin* trimmed to her most efficient point of sail in order to maximize our speed. We steered by the wind, rather than the compass. I set all of the sails with preventers, for security against accidental gybes or rogue waves, so adjusting sail trim and tacking were time-consuming jobs. Making a fast passage was important in order to minimize our potential exposure to dangerous storms, and to ensure we didn't run out of food, water, or fuel. Whenever *Dolphin's* speed fell below five knots, I would turn on the engine to add supplemental speed. Of course, the crew found this unpleasant, since it added noise, fumes, and vibration to the never-ending pitching and creaking, as well as unnecessary heat as we moved northward and away from the cold South Atlantic.

Trev and Alfie alternated four-hour helm watches around the clock. I checked our status and progress at every watch change, and recorded positional data in the log book. The helmsman had to be alert for changes in the wind direction and sea state, and for other ship traffic, as well as for potential boat problems like chafing noises or impending gear failure. Margie's main responsibility was to keep the captain and crew well fed, while rationing the ship's stores, and keeping the interior shipshape. *Dolphin* still leaked a little, even after all the repairs in Buenos Aires. The crew had to keep an eye on the depth of water in the bilges, and pump it out as necessary. In calm seas, this was only once every day or two, but in rough sailing, we needed to empty it several times a day. We recorded the number of pump strokes it took to empty the water, and I kept a watchful eye for any significant changes in the volume *Dolphin* took on. The crew took it in turn to clean and maintain the kerosene running lights. They all wanted to be sure our little craft was visible to any other ships at sea! In addition to her other duties, Margie often took a two or three hour spell at the helm in the middle of the day to give the two helmsmen a longer break, I generally enjoyed some "Captain's time," steering alone from late afternoon until dusk. We had already experienced rough conditions on our voyage from Punta Arenas to Buenos Aires, and we were ready with the warps and tires to use as drogues if necessary.

*   *   *   *   *

Navigation is the art of determining one's position on Earth within an imaginary grid of latitude and longitude lines that run horizontally and vertically around the surface of the planet. I used celestial navigation to determine our daily position in the open ocean. This can be done effortlessly these days, with Global Positioning System (GPS) devices that triangulate with geostationary satellites at fixed positions in the sky. Of course, GPS had yet to be invented in 1975, and I wouldn't have trusted it in the early days, anyway. When I set out from Los Angeles, I was determined not to rely on electronic equipment, because of its susceptibility to corrosion. Instead, I relied on a traditional sextant, and daily noon sightings of the sun, and it gave me great satisfaction that all of the remote mid-ocean rocks we were aiming for appeared on the horizon exactly where and when they were supposed to.

Landing with Réanne on Easter Island during the first leg of *Dolphin*'s voyage had been my first navigational test. The island had turned up right on schedule, thirty-two days out of Acapulco. "Pretty good, *Capitán!*" Réanne had said to me, when the small, dark mound appeared on the western horizon. "Damn right!" Easter Island was a tiny speck in the vast expanse of the South Pacific Ocean. It was both a major thrill and a considerable relief to know that I had found it—and that my navigation by sextant could be relied upon. I had taken classes in the subject at home in California before we left on our voyage, but I had few opportunities to practice before our departure. It's also a different matter using a sextant on a bouncing boat rather than standing on the beach in Santa Monica, and there are often complications like clouds, haze, and even the position of the sails, that can block the view of the horizon. (See Appendix 2 for a more detailed discussion of celestial navigation.)

The process of taking noon sightings took at least half an hour, and of course it could only be done when the sun was not obscured. After recording my sextant measurements, I would perform the necessary computations and plot our position—both latitude and longitude—on the appropriate nautical chart. I always recorded my measurements and positional fixes in Greenwich Mean Time (GMT) to remove any confusion about local time zones. On large-scale charts, our daily progress appeared to be minuscule relative to the vastness of the ocean. My sextant was a top quality (and heavy!) German instrument, with the fine scale divided into one-minute graduations (one-sixtieth of a degree, equating to about one nautical mile). At sea, highly skilled navigators can determine their position to an accuracy of about a quarter-mile. I probably didn't do as well as that, but I could reckon on being within several nautical miles of the position I marked each day on the chart—meaning we should be able to see any of the landmarks (islands, rocks, reefs etc.) which my navigation suggested we were likely to encounter along the way.

In my diary, I mused about whether navigation was a science or an art, "The art of navigation has to do with feeling good about where you are at any given point in time." I brought an additional sextant back from one of my California trips for Trev to practice with, and as he learned to use it, he observed, "The art of navigation is guessing!" The main objective was to keep my navigational uncertainties to a tolerable level. Not everything can be known, or certain, all the time, but the practiced navigator should have confidence in the amount of uncertainty achievable given the conditions.

Trev became a capable navigator by the end of the voyage. Even Margie took a turn at learning to use the sextant. I was pleased with their interest, since having a reserve navigator added a layer of safety to our voyage. Otherwise, if anything had happened to me, the crew would have been lost in the immense South Atlantic.

I confirmed my celestial navigation by supplementing it with dead reckoning (DR). This technique uses records of speed and course to compute a boat's advance from the last known position. *Dolphin* towed a mechanical log, a small device similar to a car's odometer. The mechanical log contained a rotor that spun as it moved through the water, and then it recorded each revolution. We would periodically retrieve the mechanical log, and write the number of revolutions in the logbook, converting it to distance travelled. The helmsmen also recorded the boat's compass course and wind speed hourly in the logbook. I calculated *Dolphin*'s DR position by using the compass course and recorded distance and then factoring in estimates of the current's set (direction) and drift (speed), and the boat's leeway (the downwind component of the vessel's motion). DR was particularly valuable during storms or when the sun and stars were hidden by clouds, and it served as a check on my celestial observations. The ominous name is thought to derive not from fatal miscalculation, but to be a corruption of Deduced Reckoning.

Every day, as soon as I'd worked out our position, I marked it on the chart with an "X." In these early days, all the Xs overlapped one another as we crawled eastward. The crew worked hard, changing sails to catch every puff of wind. I watched Trev working away in the middle of a night watch in the rain, hoisting sails, correcting the wheel, moving the preventers, wearing yellow foul weather gear and fighting with his safety harness as it caught on the cleats. He looked just like Sir Francis Chichester, the famous British yachtsman.

Dolphin settled into a steady operating routine. The chimes of the ship's clock ruled the helmsman's four-hour watch schedule. Each of us kept up our responsibilities, changing watches on time, and being considerate in the close quarters. The team worked well together. We all rolled up our sleeves, pitching in when necessary, and relaxing quietly when things were calm. These were wonderful days! Margie's great meals were a real morale boost as we rolled along in the light air. On some evenings, a happy hour provided another lift, as we shared a bottle or two of Argentine wine. During the days we saw nothing but the pulsing deep blue sea. The waves heaved to some distant rhythm, each wave unwinding as we slid past, nothing but the hard lined horizon against the pale sky, the same in all directions – nothing!

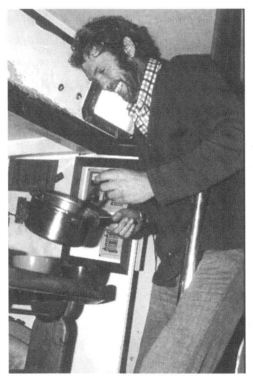

Trev cooking in Dolphin's galley

Fleets of quarter- and dime-sized Portuguese Man-o-War jellyfish drifted alongside us. Their lovely purple sails shaded to pink on the edges. They seemed to be directing their movement across the current, just like *Dolphin*. We also occasionally observed fish moving through the clear waters. Once we saw a school of sharks pursuing what looked like some kind of barracuda-type fish, driving them to jump clear of the surface to escape. Another day a formation of tuna swept past us through the sunlit water. Alfie was always eager to tow a fishing lure behind the boat. On November 25, the mechanical log got twisted in the fishing line. It took Alfie and me forty minutes to unsnarl the mess. A few days later, it happened again. We decided that this was because the lure was made by *Industria Argentina* and hence of inferior quality.

One night in the midst of this slow passage, I got a radio patch through to Réanne, who was back at her teaching job in California. Although we only chatted about trivia, it sharpened my feelings of longing for her. Margie's presence on board unsettled me, since she and Trev were so obviously in love. I expressed my own desire in explicit discussions with Trev and Alfie about how much I missed having my own lover aboard.

*   *   *   *   *

We were followed for several days by a huge dark wandering albatross. We called him White Eyes, after the white spots, or eyes, on his brown upper wings. He was with us for several days and sometimes swooped as close as 50 feet or so. It was a real thrill when he would pull up and turn sharply after a 200 yard run just inches over the water. He never landed and seldom flapped his wings—the embodiment of the beautiful and indifferent ocean.

Albatrosses   belong   to   the   biological   order *Procellariiformes*, which means "tubenoses" and includes the petrels, which have similar anatomy. They can live on the ocean for long stretches, doing without fresh water thanks to tubular structures on their upper beaks that release excess salt. The tubes also help the birds assess their flight speeds, so they can maintain prolonged dynamic soaring. Young albatrosses can reportedly remain airborne for several years without ever touching land, covering vast expanses of ocean before eventually returning to the breeding grounds where they hatched.

Insight into the diet of albatrosses comes from the study of albatross stomach contents. Albatrosses feed primarily on the fly, consuming fish, crustaceans, and cephalopods from the top three to five meters of water. Scavenged squid may be an important part of the diet. Analysis of regurgitated squid beaks shows that many of the squid were too large to have been caught alive, and some of the beaks were from deep-water squid species. The source of scavenged squid is a matter of debate. Some may come from the die-off that occurs after squid spawning, and some from the vomit of squid-eating whales. (Spare a thought for the graduate students studying this!) It appears that the two sexes of a single species may utilize separate feeding ranges. Of course, anyone who's enjoyed the opening minutes of a Nordstrom shoe sale or watched a hockey team diving into an all-you-can-eat buffet can easily imagine the reason for this segregation of the sexes.

The use of albatross as a metaphor derives from Coleridge's poem, *The Rime of the Ancient Mariner*. Someone with a burden or obstacle is said to have "an albatross around his or her neck," the punishment given in the poem to the mariner who killed the albatross. In part due to the poem, there is a widespread myth that it is unlucky for sailors to shoot or harm an albatross; in truth, sailors regularly killed and ate them, as reported by Captain Cook in 1772.

*   *   *   *   *

After five sluggish days, the wind picked up late in the evening, and we started sailing again. The barometer fell, and our position chart showed us 200 miles south of the extreme limit of icebergs. *Dolphin* screamed along, so we ran under twin headsails only with the prop howling as it came out of the water. The rail and portholes dragged through the water as the boat heeled in the waves and glowing phosphorescence streamed from her side. The seas continued to pick up, and the wet deck shone brilliantly in the moonlight. By noon the next day, the seas and wind had calmed somewhat, and we put up the reefed main for easier going.

Whatever the conditions, driving the boat was a non-stop job, requiring substantial amounts of food. Margie was mistress of the kerosene stove and prepared great meals. For example, on November 25, for breakfast we had corn flakes, powdered milk, scrambled eggs and bacon on toast, and coffee or tea. For lunch, she served string bean salad with mayonnaise, pickles, boiled eggs, cheese, chicken and fried onions on crackers, and for dinner we enjoyed mashed potatoes covered with fried onions and tomatoes, canned roast beef warmed in the skillet, boiled carrots and the remainder of the green beans. This may sound like a lot of food, but we were working hard and needed the calories to keep us fueled.

On November 28, we were roughly halfway from Buenos Aires to Tristan da Cunha Island. I started a pool on when we'd actually make landfall. Trev guessed at 1145 hours on December 8. I thought 1400 on the same day. Margie thought somewhat later, guessing 2000 on December 9. Alfie reckoned 1400 on the 10th. The small range in the guesses showed how much faith the crew had in my navigation!

By the morning of November 29, the wind again began to pick up to Force 5-6. We secured all of the movable items like seats and buckets and battened down the hatches. The boat pitched awkwardly in the heavy seas. The stove leaked kerosene, and the bilges needed more frequent pump outs. The weather was drizzly, alternating with heavy, lashing squalls. Everyone on deck clipped into safety harnesses, and Alfie took the further precaution of wearing his life jacket. It was a fast and uncomfortable ride. We had moved south of our desired track and were experiencing "Roaring Forties Syndrome," meaning that everything in the cabin was soggy, cold, and on the floor. The rain, cold winds, and lower water temperature all indicated we had sailed out of the South Atlantic current that warms as it passes along the Brazilian coast, and were now in the colder waters of the Antarctic Circumpolar Current.

The barometer began going up, but we were still sailing directly into the oncoming waves at hull speed. I needed to use the motor to overcome the backwinded main and mizzen, since getting crosswise in the huge waves by rounding up or falling off would be a disaster. I tried to get a morning sunshot but dropped and broke my watch. I couldn't get a good shot in the evening, either. The cabin seemed filled with flying objects, and I spilled my glass of wine all over the table at dinner. In spite of the challenging conditions, Margie was still fixing us hearty meals of canned meats and potatoes. I worked up my doubtful sun shots to find that they agreed pretty well with each other and with the DR calculations. This confirmed that *Dolphin*'s course had deviated southward of the plan. Since we steered relative to the wind direction and the wind had shifted from west to north, *Dolphin* was heading southeast rather than east. I needed to accept the limits of my navigational accuracy, which were broader under these difficult conditions. In any case, it was clear that *Dolphin* was too far south, and we were within about a hundred miles of the main shipping lanes. This was not good, but we needed to wait for lower seas and winds before adjusting our course.

By November 29, we had crossed latitude 38°S. Although the winds were moderate, the seas continued to worsen, with higher crests and deeper troughs. I stayed attuned to *Dolphin*'s motion as she worked the waves. However, as I was standing at the stove that evening, the boat unexpectedly took a sharp jolt and dropped right out from under me. *Dolphin* was slammed with such force that I flew across the cabin horizontally, and banged headfirst into the pump bulkhead. Margie and Trev were seated at the table and protected from the impact by the seatbacks. I was knocked unconscious, and a scalp laceration gushed blood. Frightened, but thinking quickly, Margie and Trev carried me down to the lowest point of the boat's interior, just forward of the engine compartment, to minimize the motion I experienced. Margie ordered Alfie to make sure the self-steering gear was fixed on course, and then to come inside and secure all the hatches in case of another pitchpole. *Dolphin* carried a full emergency medical kit, including scalpels, sutures and morphine, plus three different types of antibiotic medication, but of course none of that was useful in treating a concussion. Margie cleaned and bandaged my head wound, and noted that it might require stitches later. She covered me with a warm blanket, and put a pillow under my head. After some static interference, Trev managed to get a radio contact to a ham radio operator named Bill, in Johannesburg, South Africa. Bill contacted Margie's family doctor in Cape Town, and he took the call immediately when he heard that she had a medical emergency in the middle of the Atlantic Ocean. Bill relayed Dr. Stumpf's step-by-step instructions to Trev and Margie.

"Keep him warm and check his pupil dilation regularly. Concussion is usually temporary, but Don should anticipate a headache!"

Margie cradled my head on her lap as she assessed my condition and applied pressure to my scalp wound. She monitored my heart rate, and periodically peeled back an eyelid to shine a bright flashlight beam directly into my eye. She told me later that even though I was completely unconscious, the intense light caused my pupils to contract, and I would toss my head, implying that my nervous system was relatively intact. She continued talking to me, trying to get some reaction, but I remained unresponsive to her voice. No one wanted to think of the consequences if I didn't recover, leaving them without a navigator in the middle of the South Atlantic. I'm grateful that the scalp wound stopped bleeding fairly quickly. When I revived, Margie told me that if I had needed stitches, she would have asked Alfie to sew me up because he did such an excellent job mending *Dolphin*'s sails. Thankfully, stitches weren't necessary. I bear a scar in the center of my skull to this day: a quarter-sized divot testifying to the power of the Atlantic.

I roused after about three hours, but asked Trev to take charge while I recovered. The crew kept me resting in my bunk for a day, which was fine by me, since I indeed had the predicted terrible headache. As I rejoined the living, my chief concern was figuring out what had happened to us, and checking for any damage to *Dolphin*. I'm convinced that we collided with a whale. *Dolphin* had been sailing along at about five knots when the staggering blow hit us just aft of amidships, at the turn of the bilges, the very strongest part of the hull. I routinely recorded the number of pump strokes it took to empty the bilges, and the volume of water *Dolphin* took on remained unchanged after the impact. I inferred that, whale or not, the hull remained undamaged.

The next day, the mainsail suddenly backwinded in the gusty conditions. This upset a big tin of coffee in the galley, and left a huge mess for Margie to clean up. She was coming down the companionway ladder with wet boots on, and slipped and hit her head on the stowed anchor. She was pretty banged up and sore for a couple of days. Now there were two of us taking painkillers for headaches.

After I began to recover, I confirmed our position. I adjusted our course and sails to steer directly toward Tristan da Cunha. As we headed more northward, the weather improved, and we began to enjoy a little free time out of the cabin. We aired our wet clothes and shoes on deck, and listened to the shortwave radio, receiving Arabian music and a cheerful variety show from Radio Nederland. Cultural and ethnic entertainment seemed especially fine when heard in such a wild environment, so far from everything familiar. A little fresh air and relaxation really improved our attitudes. So did a bottle of Argentine dessert wine that Trev and I found. It had partly leaked around its cork into the bilges, so we finished it off. Sweet bilges! During our happy hour, I reflected on what a great crew I had found. Everyone was working hard, getting along and respecting one another. We were all teaching Alfie English, although appropriately for a sailor, most of the words in his vocabulary were obscene.

As we headed more to the northeast during that week, the weather continued to improve. I enjoyed my "Captain's time," taking the helm every afternoon as the wind freshened and the crew took siestas. It was extremely pleasurable to sit alone for several hours, musing on past and future adventures, marveling at the feel of the boat, and watching the albatross soar.

Sometimes Alfie would stick his head out of the companionway and say "Me?" He almost seemed hesitant to intrude. I would answer, "Nooo! Me!" Alfie would smile and disappear below. The boat could steer herself all afternoon while the crew slept. I even spent an afternoon washing the stove and dishes, although Margie had some choice comments on my execution since I stowed the cutlery without drying it properly, and it promptly rusted.

By December 1, we were 780 miles from Tristan da Cunha, or about six days away at our average speed of 130 miles per day. We enjoyed smooth sailing under genoa, main, and mizzen, with no engine running. Trev spotted an old yellow fender covered with barnacles, the first debris we had seen for days in that untraveled part of the world. The wind continued to lighten as we headed east, until we had no wind, only undulating swells. On December 2, we were mesmerized as the sunset put on a spectacular display. A golden thread glowed along the horizon for over an hour from due west to east of south. We all watched in silence. Alfie held his fishing line and gave periodic tugs. I longed for Réanne and pondered what my life was all about. I mused in my diary that although I could find a lot of questions in the ocean, I couldn't find many answers. We played thoughtful songs on the tape deck: *Tea for the Tillerman, Wooden Ships, Hard Headed Woman, Miles from Nowhere, Baby I Want You.* Sometimes it seemed like we were going so slowly and making such little progress, especially when I started missing Réanne. Listening to Barry White pulled my longing for her up to the surface of my thoughts. "*Never, never going to give you up!*" It was like that old sea shanty, "*It is not a leave in Liverpool that I'm a-grieving, but the thought of thee.*"

We made efficient use of every bit of wind during our passage, but even when we surfed and screamed along, the X's on the chart moved excruciatingly slowly. Tristan da Cunha *should* have just popped up over the horizon at any moment. While motoring, I sometimes got the urge to gun the throttle as if a couple of hours full out would get us there. This must have been a carry over from freeway living in California, when three or four hours with the pedal to the metal could move you 200 or 300 miles along your way. Here in the vast ocean, a full day of hard-ass work got us only about three-quarters of an inch on the pilot chart, and the scenery never varied. There was no place to hide or find protection when the squall lines bore down at breakneck speed, or when we saw sinister black clouds bleeding down into galloping cross seas, or when we were pelted by scudding torrents of driving rain. Maybe this is how patience is learned—or humility—whatever, it sure takes its sweet time in coming.

The wind returned and we flew along with full sails as we continued toward Tristan da Cunha. The weather was somewhat changeable, with rain succeeded by drizzle which then cleared into comfortable afternoons. Some little birds flew at a terrific pace barely above the water, and the wind would periodically bounce them right off the waves. I lost concentration during one tough spell at the helm and caused *Dolphin* to lurch abruptly when the sails backwinded. A jug of cooking oil fell and broke in the galley, leaving the cabin sole slippery and dangerous. Margie and Alfie rinsed and scrubbed for a long time to get it clean and safe again.

We crowded on sail as the wind slackened again. *Dolphin* began to roll in big cross seas that were caused by a combination of two wave trains. I was reminded of the large cross seas Réanne and I had fought in the Pacific. Every now and then the southwest and west waves added together to make four big waves approximately 200 feet long and fifteen feet high, about three times the height of the regular seas. They also made deep troughs ahead of the sharp wave front. The sudden sharp drops had a nerve-wracking irregularity. It was quite stressful, especially after my concussion and Margie's fall. The clouds had a strange fractured look, like dried mud in a river bottom. The light wind up the wave front picked up the small crest of the wave into a whitecap, but vanished on the other side, and the sails flapped idly as we rolled and wallowed. To add to the frustration, Alfie's fishing line caught in the mechanical log several times, which was an immense bother to untangle, especially when it never produced any fish. "Maybe *mañana*?" We still had fresh eggs, so Margie made bacon omelets. Everyone got sunburned, and Margie and I enjoyed a cooling dip in the ocean. Another wandering albatross swooped over for a few minutes and then passed on, the first bird we'd seen for a couple of days.

On the calm afternoon of December 3, I called the crew on deck to see an amazing vision surrounding our boat: innumerable brilliant jellyfish looking like electric lights in the transparent sea. We glided through them, dispersing the mass and shattering it into thousands of tiny fragments of color. The larger jellyfish floated deeper than the smaller ones on the surface. The small jelly fish had a blood red round center with golden knobs set in a circle of blue transparent jelly. The larger jellyfish had silver blue colors with shining golden knobs. They illuminated the clear ocean like a watery kaleidoscope.

Late in the night, other lights—those of the brilliant stars—reflected on the sea. I got the first good sights of the northern navigation stars since the Pacific. Rigel, Hamal, and Canopus gave me a good triangle bisected by Alpheratz, and the resulting plot put us five miles south of the DR position.

Cries of excitement awoke me at 0630 hours on December 7. Trev hollered, "Alfie! Alfie! Quick! We've got a fish!" Together, Trev and Alfie wrestled a fifteen-kilo tuna up over the rail. After the previous day's tangled mess of fishing line and mechanical log, I had almost said no more fishing, since it seemed like such a waste of time, with several hours spent unsnarling the twisted lines. The tuna this morning made up for it. Alfie was ecstatic! He had proven he was a fisherman after all the ribbing we'd given him. He attacked the carcass with gusto. Only a couple of birds were in sight, but within fifteen minutes of cleaning the fish, there were fifteen or twenty gobbling the scraps. Alfie first tied a rope around the tail so it wouldn't fall overboard, then he went to work dressing out the tuna in quick and proper fashion. He removed the head, and the tuna's many fins and spines, then scaled it, gutted it, fileted it, popped a piece into a hot pan, and served it with fresh lemon, taking only thirty minutes from dissection to digestion. Alfie purred like a kitten the entire time, "*Muy bueno, muy bueno*," and we all agreed.

That day was cool with choppy seas, but we flew along, only 300 miles from Tristan da Cunha. We drank a toast to the memory of the men who lost their lives at Pearl Harbor 35 years before. Alfie spent the afternoon reinforcing the seams in the main and staysail. We had fried tuna for breakfast, tuna with mashed potatoes and beans for lunch, and tuna stew with tomatoes, onions, and garlic for dinner. It looked like we had enough tuna for a week, and it was a great break from the canned meats Margie had been serving.

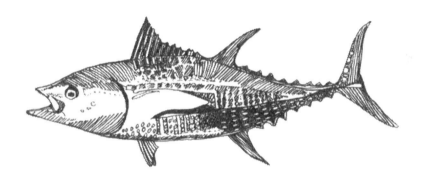

By the next morning, we had run out of stove kerosene, but this didn't worry me since we were only a day or so away from our landfall and more supplies. The weather was clear, and we flew along with eight dolphins accompanying us—the first we had seen since leaving Buenos Aires. Late that night, I thought I could distinguish a possible peak dead ahead, above the lower clouds. At 0200 hours, Trev called me topside to say, "Don, I think there's something over there." When the sun came up four hours later, Trev was nearing the end of his watch. I was up on deck drinking coffee, and, as predicted, Tristan da Cunha was visible on the horizon. Alfie was due on watch, but Trev was in no hurry to go below. It was a beautiful morning and the view of the island was spectacular. We were sure Alfie would appreciate the sight also, but on this particular morning he was late coming up on deck. When he did finally appear, he was extremely nervous until he saw Tristan looming up ahead of us. He wrapped his arms around me and kissed me sloppily on each cheek. Alfie explained that he had awakened as usual when it was his turn to go on watch, but when Trev hadn't come down into the cabin, he figured we had missed the island and were lost. He had no understanding of the mathematical principals used in navigation, or that it really was possible to determine our whereabouts from the position of the sun. *"Bueno, bueno, muy exacto! Capitán* very smart!" he declared.

Chapter 7

Tristan da Cunha to Cape Town, South Africa

9 - 22 December, 1975

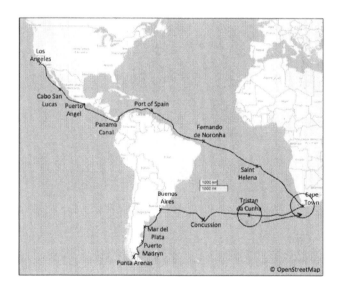

Tristan da Cunha was our only port of call in the South Atlantic Ocean between Buenos Aires and Cape Town. The name Tristan da Cunha refers to both a small archipelago of volcanic islands that collectively comprise the most remote inhabited places on earth, and to the main island in the group. The island we first approached was not Tristan itself, but Inaccessible Island, twenty-eight miles to the southwest of Tristan da Cunha Island. Inaccessible Island is a small (5.4 sq. mile) extinct volcano thought to have been named by a shipload of seventeenth-century Dutch sailors who managed to get ashore, but who failed to get beyond the beach due to the surrounding barricade of thousand-foot cliffs. Inaccessible Island may also have been named by a French captain of 1778 who failed to make landfall at all. The cliffs beyond the beach posed a problem for most of the intrepid would-be settlers who followed, from American and German sealers, to scientists and naturalists of various nationalities—although a Norwegian Scientific Expedition successfully gained access to the island's interior plateau in 1938 and catalogued the local flora and fauna. At least three ships came to grief on the island. One, the East India Company ship *Blenden Hall*, ran aground in 1821, though all but two of the 84 people aboard survived the ordeal and subsisted for several months on wild celery, seals, penguins and albatross, while they set about building boats from the wreckage of their vessel. Six people died attempting to sail to Tristan da Cunha, twenty-five miles away, but a second boat reached the larger island and the remaining survivors were eventually rescue.

Inaccessible Island is home to a number of native plant species, to fur and elephant seals, and to large colonies of seabirds. All of the archipelago's islands are part of the British overseas territory of Saint Helena, Ascension, and Tristan da Cunha, and are administered by a representative of the British Crown.

At 0645 we dropped the CQR anchor in Carlisle Bay. Alfie and I made a dinghy trip to a small pebbly beach, leaving Trev and Margie on anchor watch. Millions of shrieking seabirds filled the air, and millions more nested on every possible surface. They were astonishingly aggressive in their defense of the rocky islet. The pungent smell and deafening screams overwhelmed us as the birds attacked relentlessly. They flew right at our faces, hitting our heads and cutting through our hats with their sharp beaks, giving me a strong sensation they were targeting my eyes. I felt like an unwelcome visitor in an alien world. Although it was thrilling to be in a place that so few other humans had been, it was positively Hitchcockian, and we stayed ashore for only a few minutes.

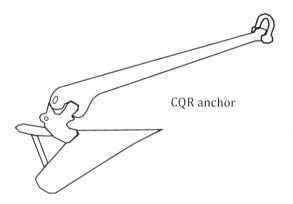

CQR anchor

We set off immediately on the five-hour sail to the main island of Tristan da Cunha. The island's 6,765-foot volcanic peak guided us to the only village, Edinburgh of the Seven Seas. We found the fishing boat *Melodie* anchored a half-mile offshore of the island's northern tip, with her crew busily unloading crates of live rock lobsters into a small motor launch acting as tender. Margie read off the echo sounder depths as we headed for

Melodie and exchanged greetings and big smiles with her crew. Their PA system blared out hit tunes in the otherwise almost silent environment. One of their selections became *Dolphin*'s unofficial anthem: "I never promised you a rose garden – along with the sunshine there has to be a little rain."

Like Punta Arenas, Tristan da Cunha is an open roadstead. The wind blows constantly around the sides of the 6,000 foot volcano, and the village lies in the only lee spot. In 1976, the actual harbor was merely a stone breakwater enclosing a small basin about thirty yards in diameter, with no room for us to enter. I asked *Melodie*'s crew where we could find a good spot to anchor. They replied that the best spot was between their boat and the breakwater, where the water was somewhat shallower. We took their advice and I dropped the CQR in eleven fathoms. Trev put the engine in reverse and the chain transmitted the sounds of the anchor bouncing along from one boulder to the next. From the racket it was making, I visualized a sea-floor made out of an old-fashioned washboard. Back we went toward the surf line, paying out more chain and wondering if the CQR would ever dig in. Finally the anchor stopped banging, the chain straightened and cut a taut line through the water. *Dolphin* came up sharply, nearly taking the bowsprit off as we finally locked into solid contact with what was probably the edge of a lava flow about sixty feet down. We all breathed sighs of relief—2,400 miles in twenty days was a reasonable spring passage halfway across the South Atlantic, and I felt proud as well as a little lucky.

The sight of the lush green vegetation and the small village directly abutting the stark black lava flows on shore appealed to us all, but it particularly fascinated Alfie. He monopolized the binoculars, excitedly giving Spanish descriptions that were mostly blown away on the brisk westerly wind. His enthusiasm was catching however, and we all wanted to go ashore to do a little exploring. I had a difficult time deciding if we had any chance of making it in the dinghy. The wind was brisk, and the entrance to the harbor appeared to break into windblown spray every few minutes. I studied *Melodie*'s launch as it made its way to the breakwater, noting that it stayed well out from shore until a set of big waves passed. Then the crew gunned the motor and entered the harbor in the aftermath of churning but harmless white foam. I thought I had figured out the wave sequence and that a pair of us might have a sporting chance to reach shore in *Dolphin*'s dinghy. On his next trip out to *Melodie*, the launch operator told me that the manager would be out for a visit shortly, so we relaxed and broke out the Old Smuggler whiskey, Argentina's most popular brand.

While we waited, *Dolphin* took on an awkward wallowing motion. The bow pointed into the prevailing west wind, and kept Dolphin parallel to the shoreline. Unhappily for us, we were also aligned parallel to the ocean swells arriving from the north. *Dolphin* rolled deeply with each wave, adding to our eagerness to reach the comfort of dry land. Each of us talked about the things we hoped to find on shore: fresh vegetables, fruit, lamb, a bath, and all the other things we had been missing.

Presently a second small launch appeared from behind the breakwater with three people aboard. They were all wearing life jackets. One man was wearing a tweed coat, white shirt and tie, and he seemed to be in charge. He yelled, "May I come aboard?" which sounded more like a plea for help than a request for permission. I hollered back, "Of course, but be careful!" On his first attempt at boarding amidships, the man got one foot onto *Dolphin*, but as Trev and I grabbed one arm, he yelled "let go" and fell back into the arms of the launch crew. The problem was that the boats weren't rolling in unison. One deck would be several feet above the other for a brief moment before violently reversing in the other direction. The launch crew fell off to try approaching from the stern instead, but got caught under the overhang, and *Dolphin* received two big scars as the steel launch crashed into her wooden hull. The launch crew tried another attempt at the quarter and *Dolphin* took an unusual deep roll, almost a lurch, to port. The bow of the launch hit the mizzen mast's standing rigging, and broke the fiberglass man-overboard pole.

The tweed-clad official finally made it aboard with a headfirst dive over the lifelines as Trev and I hauled at his belt and the seat of his pants. I said a rather feeble, "Welcome aboard" as he grabbed at the handrail on the cabin and sat down to catch his breath. The launch crew yelled to Alfie to pay out the line and cast it off so that they could stand off down wind. Alfie stood there repeating *"No entiendo nada!"* ("I don't understand!") This didn't faze the crew and they kept yelling "Tie us off the stern, matey," and "Let us fall off behind." Communication was at a very low level all around, and *Dolphin* was taking a fearsome pounding as the hulls crashed together. Seeing the manager safely seated and holding on for dear life, I grabbed the boat hook and attempted to push the launch away before we were holed on the spot. Alfie had a death grip on their bow line and wasn't going to let go or give an inch. Using sign language, Trev got the helmsman to put the launch in reverse and back away while I bent another line to the short bow line and convinced Alfie to move to the stern cleat and pay out some line.

The immediate threat of going to the bottom of the Atlantic had passed and we turned our attention to our visitor. He was rapidly regaining his composure after pulling his life jacket down from his neck and straightening out his good Scottish tweeds. We all went below and had a whiskey and water before talking further. Our new passenger introduced himself as "Stan Trees, Island Administrator for Her Majesty's Colonial Service." I was a little taken back, since this was the first time I had ever been in the presence of an honest to goodness imperialist. I thought by now colonialists existed only in history books and in the east/west rhetoric of the United Nations, but we all quickly relaxed. Unlike the officials I'd met in Argentina and Uruguay, Mr. Trees wasn't carrying a submachine gun or even a pistol on his belt, and we outnumbered him four to one. I reported to him we had briefly landed earlier at Inaccessible Island, and that we had left everything completely untouched. I requested a belated permission to land there. He took a deep breath, gathered strength from all corners of the empire where the sun never sets, and bellowed, "Permission granted!"

Mr. Trees approaching *Dolphin* with *Melodie* in the background.

After our introductions, Mr. Trees asked if we needed anything. I thought he couldn't have been better trained by the California Chamber of Commerce. We told him we really didn't need much, but that we would like a little diesel fuel, water, kerosene, and perhaps some fresh produce, if it wasn't too much trouble. He advised against using *Dolphin*'s little dinghy and said he would have the cannery manager send out the launch to fetch us the next morning at any hour we named. We quickly said 8 a.m. He also told us that wearing life jackets was the law of the island. He said he would give us two or three cabbages from his own garden, and we could probably buy eggs since almost everyone kept chickens.

*   *   *   *   *

Tristan da Cunha is the most remote inhabited island in the world, meaning the settlement is farthest from any other habitation. At the time of our visit in 1975, it was even more isolated, as generally only two regular supply ships called per year. We were only the second transit boat to call at Tristan da Cunha in six months. The previous boat was *Dolphin of Leith*. She had arrived about two weeks before after a forty-three day passage from Buenos Aires. The port authorities noticed them sitting off the island's coast for almost five hours without making any progress toward the harbor, so a launch was sent out to tow them in. Several commercial boats stopped in Tristan a few times a year to pick up frozen rock lobster for delivery to Cape Town. The small local boats fished for only seventy-five days out of the year, due to the challenges in getting out of the harbor. Frozen rock lobster made up the island's the entire commercial output. The economy was simple, since the plant had a standing order for all the rock lobster they could pack. At the time of our visit, there was no real port, just a small breakwater. A crane lifted the small fishing boats up onto shore for protection from the wild ocean.

The volcano that formed the island was last active in 1961. That eruption destroyed the rock lobster processing facility, and lava flows threatened the town. The entire population was evacuated by ship, although almost everyone chose to return after several years in South Africa and England. The population at the time of our visit was approximately 300 people, descended from about fifteen original settlers. The eighty or so Tristan families share only eight surnames. As might be expected on an island with a limited population and a prolonged period of intermarriage, some health problems are endemic, including asthma and glaucoma. The islanders had buried one citizen in the last week, and there had also been one birth. Six British government employees lived on the island: Mr. Trees, the doctor, education, agriculture, and engineering officers, and a radio officer who was presently on leave. There were no taxes or unemployment. My respect for the efficiency and civility of British officialdom quickly increased, as Mr. Trees brought all of the entry forms to be filled out in quadruplicate, and carried enough stamps and ink to endorse everything in sight. He never demanded our documents, and he inflicted no bureaucratic delays like we'd experienced in Puerto Madryn.

Margie and Trev had a friend, Bill van Ryssen, who was actually on Tristan at that time. Bill was a South African wildlife photographer working on a book about South Atlantic birds, and they'd contacted him before we left Buenos Aires. Bill and Mr. Trees had taken tea together just the day before, and he had told Mr. Trees all about our voyage. Bill took the dynamic picture of Dolphin leaving Tristan da Cunha used on the cover of this book.

As his next official act, Mr. Trees handed me a sack of "Her Majesty's Mail," with a specific request to hand it *personally* to the postmaster in Cape Town and no one else. No mail had left the island since early October, so we were providing a real service to the isolated community. I felt truly honored to be entrusted with this mission.

Margie brought out a can of peanuts and we sipped Old Smugglers whiskey while we chatted. The islanders called Mr. Trees "the manager," while he called himself the administrator. After years of colonial service in the Falkland Islands, he had retired for two years and then asked for reassignment, and was still in his first year on Tristan. He invited us for a drink at his office the next day, and then we got a "cheerio" and reversal of the boarding process.

It was now late afternoon, so we settled down for what we hoped would be a comfortable night, but we certainly didn't get one. On the contrary, all four of us agreed that it was one of the worst nights ever, and that we would rather be on the open seas. *Dolphin* rolled from beam end to beam end. I opened the curtains on my berth to throw out a Kleenex and got a bucketful of water on my bunk. No one could find a comfortable position.

In the middle of the night, I put up the mizzen sail to try and stabilize the hull, but then later awoke wondering if we might sail right into the cliffs and breakers just a hundred yards or so away. The racket was unbelievably loud. The anchor chain rubbing up and down across the lava sounded and felt like someone was taking a crude rasp file to the hull, removing half an inch of wood on each stroke. There was nothing that could be done about it. I was afraid to shorten the chain because we might dislodge the anchor, so the rubbing went on and on. I couldn't sleep because I worried that the chain would foul on the lava and that on any swell the chain could snap right in two. In addition, every half hour or so, we were rocked by a williwaw, or high-velocity gust, caused by the winds funneling down the volcanic cliffs. These gusts came at a right angle to the regular winds, causing all kinds of disruption. They caught the mizzen sail and laid *Dolphin* over on her seaward side, then rotated her until the stern faced the charging swells. These hit the flat transom with a mighty bang, sending the boat surging forward until the anchor chain came up tight under the bobstay, then the chain would slip along link by link, as if the bowsprit was next to go. The boat either took a beating by the bow and stern, or else she wallowed broadside, throwing around everything that wasn't screwed down tight.

At dawn, the seas had an even uglier appearance and a trip ashore seemed questionable. We put on clean clothes and got ready just in case. At 0800 hours, the harbor crane put the small launch back in the water and two guys quickly ran out to us. The cannery manager had recommended they fill our diesel and water jugs for us, but I pushed for a brief trip ashore. Trev volunteered to go and do what he could while they filled the tanks. He tried twice to get aboard the launch but he nearly pinned his leg between our deck and the launch's stern, so I called off the venture. It was just too risky. Instead, we threw our water, kerosene, and diesel drums across and one of the men caught them all, even though between our bad tosses and the tremendous gusts, they bounced all around the launch.

As the launch returned to the harbor, I evaluated their performance, imagining I was on board too, although I was very glad I wasn't. These sailors were good: they looked like pictures of the U. S. Coast Guard lifeboat crew bashing through the heavy surf over the shallow entrance bar at the mouth of the Columbia River. Three times they gunned the engine and started in across the last hundred yards, but three times they aborted their attempt at the last possible second, pushing the tiller hard over and spinning the launch on a dime, heading out to deeper water to try another approach. At times, the launch completely disappeared from our view as the waves topped six to eight feet. On the fourth attempt, the launch made it and came to a screaming stop at the sea wall. At this point I wished I had just thanked them for their trouble and had not asked them to bring us the fuel and water. I figured we might stay an hour or two to see if the wind calmed down a bit so they could get back out to us, but if it increased, we would just raise the anchor and head out to sea for Cape Town.

In spite of my doubts, the launch crew loaded the jugs immediately and in thirty minutes were back alongside *Dolphin*.

The swells tossed both boats so violently that we didn't even consider getting close alongside the launch. Instead, each of the water bottles, kerosene cans, and the two diesel drums were tied to lines, dropped into the water and hauled across to bring on board. We could handle just one jug at a time. This meant that the launch had to make a fresh approach and we had to heave our line back across for each and every container. It was an extremely time consuming job and required the most careful seamanship and small-boat handling.

I started *Dolphin*'s engine and tried heading into the waves to decrease the rolling in the troughs, but the bow kept blowing off to one side or the other, and that proved to be more of a hindrance than a help. Getting the first eleven gallon diesel drum aboard was quite a challenge. When Alfie, Trev, and I finally got it on deck, it slid all over the place, so I decided to take it directly below. By the time the drum reached the bottom step of the ladder, a seam had opened up and heavy dark diesel was pouring everywhere—all over the steps, engine box, life preservers, the stove, the floor, everywhere! Standing up became impossible as everything was slick. We had all been wearing clean clothes and shoes in anticipation of the trip ashore and now everything was wet, slippery, and filthy.

We warned the launch not to attempt another pass. After getting a couple more ropes around the leaking drum, we got it back up on deck, where it was just as slick down below, and tied it to the stern pulpit. The situation was becoming serious and it

Making the fuel transfer at Tristan da Cunha

was clear that one of us could get injured unless something was done. We had to get the dangerously slippery cabin floor cleaned up. Trev found a solution by taking his clothes off and sitting on the floor, sliding from one side of the cabin to the other while he partially washed the cabin down, wiping the fuel into the bilges. I was heartily thankful for our diesel engine. Spilled gasoline and our running engine would have blown us sky high.

Somehow Alfie and I got the remaining fuel drums aboard and stowed below with a minimum of damage. The split drum couldn't be left to leak all over the deck, so Alfie and Trev hand-pumped what was left through a filter and into the main tank. In the meantime, I sent across a thank you note and payment to Mr. Trees for the fuel, with tips for the excellent seamen in the launch. They were cheerful and friendly and wished us a good voyage. We couldn't watch their return trip to the harbor because it took every amount of concentration to keep us from being bashed to death. We sloshed bucket after bucket of saltwater both above and below decks until finally our shoes began to grip the non-skid deck once again.

The crew sang *Dolphin's* new theme song, "We got to get out of this place," as we attempted to hoist the anchor. Not surprisingly, the rugged basalt beneath us had firmly captured the CQR, and *Dolphin* was stuck solid. Normally, driving the boat directly over the anchor tightens the chain, and when the boat rises to a swell it will pull the anchor free, but that didn't work at Tristan. The bowsprit flexed uncomfortably and finally the chain jumped clear from the windlass drum. *Dolphin* shuddered violently. I had made up my mind I didn't want to leave the CQR at Tristan, but it was too rough and dangerous to launch the dinghy and attempt to get a second line worked down to the bottom in order to try a backwards pull. Only brute force would solve this one. I put the engine full speed ahead and overran the anchor chain to strain it from a different direction. I got the same result each time, as the chain strained to the verge of breaking and then sprang free of the windlass and paid out several feet, releasing the pressure. Finally I found the right direction of pull and the anchor came free. We cut off the mass of seaweed entangled in the chain and got everything aboard and stowed.

It was almost noon when we finally got the main and staysails up and waved goodbye to the onlookers on shore, including a row of school children waving white handkerchiefs. It was good to be heading out to open sea again. Initially I set a course directly north to clear the williwaws and reach the prevailing westerly wind ASAP. However, the winds appeared fluky, so I gybed to the east and drove downwind along the shore under mainsail alone. The wind whistled along eastbound under the nearby lava cliffs. The crew went below to change into clean, dry clothes, have some coffee, and warm up.

Within five minutes, the wind had increased sharply. The boat took off flying and I let out a yodel when the knotmeter pegged at ten knots. The helm became very stiff and I had to crank the wheel completely to port to try and overcome *Dolphin*'s strong tendency to steer into the direction of the wind. The load on the rudder bearings, shaft and gearbox must have been terrific. If I had tried to turn the wheel any faster I think I might have broken off the wooden handholds. This was the stiffest I had ever felt the helm, and as the wind kept increasing to full gale intensity it became obvious that *Dolphin* was completely overpowered and had way too much sail up. Worse, I was slowly losing ground at the helm, and if this kept up I wouldn't be able to prevent the boat from being knocked down, or even rounding up and broaching. The main boom was let out only about halfway to the normal running position, and *Dolphin* was heeling ever more deeply and going even faster. With the center of sail now far outboard to port, there was an extremely strong force-couple causing her to point ever higher into the wind, and straight at the cliffs. Heeled almost onto her side, *Dolphin* was totally ignoring her rudder!

The boat shuddered from bow to stern and laid her lee deck further and further under water. I continued to crank more and more helm to port, trying to get the boat back under control. My efforts succeeded only in keeping the boat from broaching. Unless the wind lightened and I could release the sails, we would be up against the lava cliffs in one or two minutes. I could only wonder if we would lose the mast or sails if the boat lay all the way over at our current speed, which could have been as much as fifteen knots.

About this time the wheel hit the stop, and I knew there was no hope of overcoming the weather helm. I cried, "All hands, all hands!" The main hatch opened and Trev and Alfie scrambled out. The critical point had arrived, and we had to act immediately. The only thing we could do fast enough was to release the main sheet and let the mainsail feather into the wind. I yelled directions to Trev, but since I couldn't get the helm over any more I let go of the wheel and sprang forward to release the main sheet myself. Removing the hitch allowed the sheet to uncleat itself, and it went flying out through the blocks. Only the preventer kept the boom from doing serious damage to the shrouds. The effect was immediate and dramatic. The port deck reappeared out of the water, the rudder began to work, and the bow slowly moved away from the looming cliffs. *Dolphin* had narrowly escaped destruction on the volcanic cliffs. As we passed Big Point, the wind became a stiff breeze. Trev rethreaded the main sheet through the five port blocks and we proceeded east. I was relieved we hadn't been sailing with any of the headsails up at the time, as I likely couldn't have recovered control.

Margie holding some of the fine rock lobster tails.

Our new course took us slowly away from the island. Once we rounded Big Point, we would be pointing directly toward Cape Town. Only about a mile ahead, Big Point itself was an impressive sight, with its nearly sheer vertical walls rising straight out of the sea and disappearing into the clouds about 1,500 feet above us. As conditions eased and I regained control, the crew returned below hollering "Take it easy, Pally!" followed by "You'll get a whack on the ear for the likes of that!" Then Margie yelled up that she had opened the box we received along with the fuel and water. It contained a couple of dozen fresh rock lobster tails. It was a wonderful gift from the cannery manager along with a note and best wishes for a good voyage.

The value of an aft cockpit was apparent. I could watch the windsock at the top of the mast and see the entire mainsail at a glance. I remembered the advice of Woody Blondfield, my former engineering manager and flight instructor back in California. He constantly emphasized that under emergency conditions it was imperative to keeping your eyes moving, and not let them stare at any one instrument or airplane part. I took quick peeks to verify that our compass heading wasn't changing, glanced at the sails and telltales, and checked the knot meter. The knotmeter pegged again, not bouncing off the pin, but forced against the limit as if glued in place.

Everything seemed to be going well at last. I yelled out triumphantly to the natural world and to the crew below that *Dolphin* had reached the pinnacle of high performance sailing. "All the sailors down in Davy Jones's locker and all the ships at sea should beware, because this *Dolphin* is the most perfect ship afloat, and she can sail under any challenge in this bloody ocean!"

But for all my gusto and cockiness, I almost sailed her under, right there off Big Point.

Trev had taken care to leave the main boom full out, and to tighten the preventer hard. As the wind increased, *Dolphin* sailed faster and faster. I relaxed a little, as I could keep the bow running directly downwind with only moderate helm pressure to port, even though the helm was extremely stiff. If the wind's direction and speed held constant, we would be a mile or so offshore and well outside the kelp in just a few minutes.

The wind direction did hold more or less constant, but the velocity increased above gale force. Huge boils swirled across the water surface, and sea smoke blew fiendishly from astern. Our speed created such big bow and quarter waves that it appeared as if we were riding down a white carpet. We *were* riding down all right—down deeper and deeper into the water. Maybe my taunting had awakened Davy Jones's men and they were pulling us down to join them! I had read of great clipper ships, caught before a gale with too much canvas flying, that had actually sailed the bow under, usually with devastating results to rigging, ship, and crew.

In fact, *Dolphin* had settled a good foot below her normal water line while screaming along downwind. In spite of my growing anxiety, I found this fascinating, because the boat had been designed with tremendous reserve buoyancy. Her designer, William Garden, had given her a large stern overhang and high flaring freeboard forward. At our pre-departure open house in Los Angeles, I noticed that with over thirty people on board at once, a load of 5,000 pounds, *Dolphin* had only settled about four inches down into the water. Now I could see that only a foot or less of freeboard remained, which meant *Dolphin* was experiencing a downwind force from the mizzen and main sails of more than 10,000 pounds!

With no apparent tendency to broach, there appeared to be no immediate danger, and I was simply awestruck at the thrilling situation. This was one of those rare moments of supreme sailing, when the physical relationships between the sailor, the boat, the wind, and the sea become almost spiritual. All of the elements and the total environment merged into unity, with everything working to perfection in dynamic harmony.

The fine edge between high performance and failure, good judgment or foolishness, success or disaster, likewise merged into a single point. This point became the focus of all my concentration, and consumed all of the physical and mental power I could summon. Adding to the thrill was the knowledge that all of *Dolphin*'s safety factors, all of the design margins for unanticipated conditions, were being used up and the point of failure and destruction was at hand.

Dolphin continued to plow through the water as if driven by a thousand horsepower. Was I so fascinated by the experience that I'd become paralyzed and incapable of action? The mainsail was spread flat against the starboard shrouds and the spreader. Each baggy wrinkle poked through in high relief. Surely the wind had to ease any second. I thought again of William Garden's beautiful design. He would have been thrilled to see his boat taking all this wind, with nothing deforming except the strong rigging and tight sheets. But as I felt the wind increasing to well over gale force, I realized that something had to give. The boat settled even deeper into the water, perhaps two feet below her waterline, equivalent to 25,000 lbs. or more. *Dolphin* could have stabbed her bowsprit into a swell at any moment. We had passed the vanishing point of high performance sailing into the mighty unknown, and its partner, terror, was about to come on board.

I yelled out with another "All hands!" At the same moment, the taut preventer on the main sail gave way with a loud report. The main boom sprang upward like a giant erection. The imminent danger was now completely obvious: if the wildly gyrating boom were thrown across to the other side in an accidental gybe, the mast and rigging would certainly all carry away overboard. I absolutely had to keep the wind off a dead run and toward the starboard quarter, but without broaching. My options were very limited at this point. I had to be completely responsive to the smallest change in the wind direction and *Dolphin*'s heading.

Trev was the first to hit the deck. He went for the broken preventer, but the stainless steel shackles at the top of the five-part block and tackle had broken completely off. I sent Alfie forward to drop the mainsail: *"¡Abajo la vela! ¡Rapido!"* ("Lower the sail! Quick!") The swinging boom threatened to make a Chinese-junk style jib no matter what I did on the helm. The mainsail's top six sail slides had given way, and the mainsail began to pull away from the mast. Alfie released the main halyard but nothing happened. We didn't have many more seconds before the boat became unstable—we had to get the goddamn mainsail down fast. Alfie started clawing the main down, but the wind pressure glued it to the rigging. Trev worked his way forward to help Alfie. I yelled again in both English and Spanish to get the main down. I was on the verge of panic—we were all on borrowed time. Trev stood on the dinghy, leapt up, grabbed the mainsail luff as high up as he could and put his full 6'2" frame and weight behind getting the sail down. It moved a few inches and he repeated the process, again and again. Meanwhile, more sail slides gave way, and a three foot long rip opened up along the leach. Trev and Alfie continued to wrestle the sail down, and *Dolphin* stopped trying to bury herself in the churning waves.

Just as Alfie and Trev got the mainsail down, we sailed out of the kelp patch and the seas started tossing us around like a plastic bathtub toy. This was unpleasant, but with the sail down, I was back in control. While we'd been racing across the kelp patch, the kelp had saved us by dampening the waves, preventing them from breaking across us. Although *Dolphin* was being forced downward, the bow hadn't been forced under, I'd responded quickly enough to avoid getting backwinded, and the mast hadn't failed. We had recovered in the nick of time. What a farewell to the fog-shrouded, williwaw-ravaged island of Tristan de Cunha!

*   *   *   *   *

Conditions calmed as we drew further into the open ocean, away from the turbulent winds and seas that the defended the island. We were able to relax and appreciate the gift of fresh rock lobster for supper (and for several subsequent breakfasts, lunches, and dinners as well!) I fixed evening cocktails on the fantail to celebrate our narrow escape, and we enjoyed an appropriate rendition of *Stormy Weather* from Radio Nederland. The short wave radio picked up world news in dialect from the Voice of the Gospel in Addis Ababa, and heard Radio North Korea's diatribe against the US imperialists and the South Korea puppets who were ignoring the patriotic people's wishes under the red flag of the three revolutions. It seemed awfully distant from our little wooden world. That night we all collapsed into bed while the helmsmen steered under the stars.

We spent an easy day on December 11, since the boat and crew all needed to recover from the ordeal the previous twenty-four hours. Curious dolphins accompanied us for a few hours. They behaved more shyly than I was used to, seldom surfing the bow wave, but rather darting across our path and quickly falling back. Our routine ran as smoothly as before with watches changing on time, excellent meals, and easy progress.

Later that day, I tried to contact Cape Town via ham radio but had no luck. The weather stayed fair, with good winds, and we enjoyed smooth and fast sailing. *Dolphin* had run 2,500 miles since Buenos Aires. We started another pool for our Cape Town arrival. The estimates were all within twenty-four hours of each other. I'm sure my accurate landfall on Tristan da Cunha strengthened the crew's confidence in my navigational skills.

The intense experience of sailing *Dolphin* to her absolute limits compelled me to write about it while my observations were still fresh. I wanted to capture my raw feelings about driving *Dolphin* to the razor's edge of catastrophe to achieve the glory of maximum performance:

*   *   *   *   *

A wooden machine, with sails feeling the air, a keel pressing the water, and humans working aboard, moves across the ever-changing surface of the planet in time to rhythms as old as the heavens and as new as each sun rise. Part of the joy I get from sailing is the feeling when the boat presses ahead under full sail, meeting and taking the seas in a constant smooth and surging fashion; the bow parts each wave, rolling and raising with each swell, leaving behind a line of popping bubbles and swirling eddies.

The sheets strain to check the taut canvas as it snares the attacking wind, heeling the boat to leeward. The wind's forward component transforms to a force powering the boat ahead, then the wind slides off the sail to fall off downwind and catch up with its counterparts. The process is unending. As a consequence of the dynamically balanced forces, the hull is held steady about the roll axis as the boat reaches across the wind, and the predominant motion is a gentle pitching up and down of the bow as waves pass from windward to leeward in never ending rows. If the wind is moderate and the boat well balanced, the helm takes care of itself without a finger being lifted for hours on end. Time after time, with a single nod of the bowsprit and a slight fluttering of the sail leach, the hull accommodates each ocean wave. Met, measured, and accommodated with complete satisfaction and a natural efficiency, a simplicity that defies human understanding.

In running before a storm the scene is vastly different. The wind in the rigging tells the story. The pressure of wind against anything in its path increases as the square of its velocity. With rising winds, even the smallest rope, cable, or square inch of sailcloth quivers and vibrates. The entire ship resonates to the tune the wind plays. In the protection of a swell, you can think, but when the boat is riding over the crest, the wind sucks your breath away, and the rushing noise obliterates all thought. However, it is the sea that destroys. The wind can shriek and howl all it wants over a well-found boat, but let the seas smash down onto the shell of a hull and something must give. Water is incompressible, therefore the boat must yield. If the hull holds together, it maintains its buoyancy and floats, evading the crushing load in the most unpredictable and unstable ways. There are a few general principles. If the water in the form of a wave or tumbling crest hits the bow, the boat pitches up violently with a shudder to its very deepest timbers. Off the bow there is a loud slap with great volumes of water flowing along the topside and spray blowing aft more than 10 feet above the deck. A direct broadside blow causes a deep lurch and skidding motion off downwind and a sinking feeling in your stomach. The curvature of the hull known as the turn of the bilges forces the mass of water to flow over the deck, up the cabin sides, and across the roof, filling every hole, opening, or hollow it can find.

Some observers find quartering the seas to be the best attitude in rough water. The resulting motion produces all of the previous sensations, but the consequences are sometimes lessened since the boat is moving in the direction of the approaching water. Taking the seas on the stern quarter has one esthetically pleasing reward. The boat's forward surging and leeward heeling causes a big bow wave to be thrown downwind. The flying water, the tumbling white foam racing to get out of the way, and the subsequent popping of millions upon millions of white bubbles as they rush by are sights and sounds to remember. When cross seas are running, the boat frequently smashes from left to right through spray and solid water onto both sides, so the effect is like a giant white pathway across the seas. The motion is similar to a skier on a steep slope, as he reduces his speed by slaloming sharply from left to right and back again.

When an ugly sea builds up and presents an onrushing slope every bit as menacing as an icy descent to the skier, all the weather-beaten skipper can do is turn tail and hope for the best. Surely this wall of water will fall vertically upon the deck and end the boat's misery. As it towers above the helmsman, poised to strike, the little craft's stern somehow, almost magically, rises to the call. Soon boat, breaking crest, and all are screaming forward at breakneck speed. Big-wave surfers know the feeling—"what the hell am I doing here?" The bow points straight down and surely any moment the freeboard will disappear into the snarling foam as the crest rushes past. As the wave loses its hold and passes ahead, you find your boat sitting in a large blanket of frothy white foam, wondering in a rather dazed and shell-shocked fashion: would I really rather be sailing? Sometimes the dream of a lifetime is really a nightmare.

*   *   *   *   *

Over the next few days the sun shone. We washed our clothes, repaired the sails and rigging, and performed general maintenance. Trev noticed a three foot long split down the length of the keel-stepped main mast between the cabin ceiling and floor. It must have been caused by compression loading when *Dolphin* sailed right under. Clearly the tremendous forces we'd experienced had damaged her, but not to the point of failure. The list of damages was long, and while we could make some repairs at sea, we would just have to monitor other items. I didn't feel the need to take immediate action on the crack in the main mast, but that evening Trev noticed it had widened. I added that to my list of repairs and routine checks:

1) Repair the mainsail slides and rips
2) Tighten the loose head stays
3) Put the shackle back on the jib
4) Rig a new preventer on the mainsail
5) Sew a patch on mizzen staysail
6) Tighten the prop shaft packing gland
7) Remove and stow the CQR
8) Recheck chronometer time
9) Bring DR plots up to date
10) Keep a watchful eye on the cracked main mast

We crossed the Prime Meridian on December 14: zero degrees longitude. We celebrated at 1300 with gin and orange juice. A thin, smoky haze obscured the horizon, which Trev facetiously declared had come all the way from Greenwich, England. Later we enjoyed calm seas and lovely sunset. The crew was heartened to hear that we had sailed 2,910 out of 3,800 miles to Cape Town. The easy swells and constant wind bore us steadily east.

*   *   *   *   *

Alfie maintained a consistently cheerful mood, while the rest of us experienced fluctuating emotions and occasionally became irritable. We weren't usually annoyed with each other specifically, but we all suffered from a bit of cabin fever. One person's bad mood quickly spread through the rest of the crew, and the close quarters wore away our tolerance for little annoyances—how many times the water pump was used for a glass of water or if someone had left the water tap half way up. All of the fresh provisions had run out and we now had only canned fruits and vegetables. Everyone was a bit short of sleep and craving sugar as well, adding to the edginess. Each of us found individual ways to cope with the close quarters. Margie's favorite quiet time "escape" was to sit on the foredeck, propped against a sail bag reading, eating cookies, sun tanning or simply falling asleep to the lull of the waves. I enjoyed several swims, both for physical refreshment and for a change of perspective.

I continued to work the ham radio, and one day connected with two amateur radio operators in Cape Town. Both men reported that the city's great landmark, Table Mountain, was draped with a white cloud, the famous "tablecloth," and that the strong and blustery offshore wind South Africans call "the Cape doctor" was charging down the slopes and out to sea. I tried to patch through to Margie's family in Cape Town but it was Friday night and everyone was out. The operators offered to phone Margie's parents the next day and to look out for us on the bandwidth the following week.

By December 16, we were only 700 miles from Cape Town. We hadn't seen any albatross in several days. Instead there were lots of small gulls with black wings. We also began to see flying fish. The small blue creatures zipped up from the surface to land on *Dolphin*'s deck; one even made it through a porthole into my bunk. One morning, while Alfie was taking a leak, he spotted two whales a mile or two north. He seemed to have a consistent problem in deciding which side of the boat was the lee and appropriate to use. Almost every morning we'd hear him exclaim "Noooooo! Arrgh!" His sense of humor was unimpaired, and he could laugh at himself along with the rest of us.

The port water tank ran dry, so we switched to the starboard, which was only about half full. I noticed a large puddle of water on the floor, but I couldn't tell if it was fresh or salt. It could have been leakage from a freshwater tank, or seawater from the bilges or our gear. We seemed to be consuming fresh water at a much faster rate since our stop at Tristan da Cunha, but I wasn't sure if the water was leaking away, or if the crew were being wasteful. They began acting as if our landfall was just around the corner, which annoyed me since we still had almost a week of sailing to go.

As we continued to eastward, the winds began to die. The weather stayed war, although the skies were grey and the swells were disorganized and irregular. The seas looked like a silver-grey bedspread draped over a restless sleeper as they heaved and tossed in a confused fashion. We motored steadily after spending three hours transferring diesel to the main tank in a sloppy manner that made a huge mess. Trev and I worked up our afternoon celestial observations with similar results that both disagreed with the DR log. I determined to head a bit northerly to avoid any risk of being carried past Africa's southern tip.

On the afternoon of December 19, the engine came to a lurching stop with a horrible grinding noise. I peered over the transom and saw a piece of heavy cargo net trailing beneath us. At this point, Margie truly earned her passage. She was a gutsy young woman generally full of common sense, and in great shape. She saw the problem, immediately grabbed some goggles and the machete we kept in the cockpit, peeled off all her clothes, and dove overboard to hack through the netting. *Dolphin* was still moving at about three knots, and I saw that Margie was in danger of getting left behind. I grabbed some line from the cockpit, dove in alongside, and tied Margie and myself off to stanchions. The ball of netting had melted and fused itself around the engine shaft, about six feet under water. Margie and I took turns sawing at it, carefully handing the sharp knife to one another. Margie figured out that it was more effective to saw along the length of the shaft rather than across it so we could peel the snarl away. We had sawed for more than an hour, and the sky was growing dark by the time we freed the propeller. I greatly admired Margie's initiative and accomplishment, not to mention the fact that she'd thought to remove her clothes so she wouldn't have to wear them brine-soaked and sticky afterwards.

Apart from that net and a few plastic bottles, we observed very little debris as we travelled. For a time, the water teemed with big patches of red plankton. It took us about six hours to sail through the mess before the sea regained its pristine aquamarine tint. Later we enjoyed the company of a pair of dolphins for several hours, which made up for not having seen any albatross for several days. I finally got some good star shots with the sextant, and the computations agreed with the morning's sun shot.

On the radio, BBC reported that the Argentine Air Force had revolted and seized three bases and three radio stations. During my stay, I had felt that Argentina was on a political precipice, and now the revolution had started. In the evening, I was able to get a complicated radio relay through to Margie's family in Cape Town. The operator spoke to a ham radio operator in Jerusalem, who relayed a message from Margie to an operator in Rio de Janeiro. The next operator relayed the message to someone in Johannesburg, and that operator held a phone to the radio while Margie's parents and sister Barbara listened to Margie's message. We heard their voices, although the elaborate process compressed the sounds into chattering squeaks. It was an extremely convoluted process, but it worked surprisingly well.

The appearance of increasing amounts of debris in the water and flying insects on board indicated that we were drawing near land. Alfie and Trev caught another small tuna, which provided a welcome change from our canned fare. There was nothing better than fish that went from hook to frying pan in fifteen minutes. Later that day, I dropped and broke the thermometer. Alfie had never seen mercury, and he was fascinated. Clean up was challenging, but I eventually managed by wetting the floor with salt water, shaking flour over it, then scraping up the resulting mess with tissue. Trev was able to pull in a Cape Town FM radio station, so we knew we were really getting close to landfall. We heard from BBC that the Argentine Air Force was buzzing the capitol buildings, and that the state of siege was continuing into a second day. Once again I was glad we had left Argentina when we did.

The longest day of the year in the Southern Hemisphere, Sunday, December 21, brought us almost eighteen hours of daylight here at 34°S. *Dolphin* was flying along again, although as the wind continued to rise we had to stow the genoa and reduce sail to just the staysail and mizzen. The seas were building and breaking, but the water remained surprisingly clear. Trev, Alfie, and I wore slickers and boots as the waves began to break over *Dolphin*'s bow, pouring water around the hatch seams. The ride was choppy and bouncy with lots of spray. The wind rose to Force 6, and we pounded along heavily. The navigation plot showed our position at 150 miles southwest of Cape Town. Sun sights were certainly easier in these warm, sunny conditions, even with the strong winds and boisterous ride!

On Monday morning, December 22, we sighted Table Mountain dead ahead. We replaced the working jib with the genoa and hoisted the mizzen in addition to the main. We all freshened up for our arrival, putting on blue jeans and our red *Le Dauphin Amical* team jerseys. Alfie washed his hair and shaved, and even put on aftershave. Trev and I settled for washing, and Margie put on lipstick and a dab of perfume. Look out, Cape Town, here we come! The strong southeasterly wind forced us away, and we had to beat into the harbor with the staysail, mizzen, and full engine power. Two men motored out in a launch to bring us all in to clear Customs. Since *Dolphin* flew the American flag, the men assumed none of us spoke Afrikaans, the second official language of South Africa. The men looked Margie over and spoke of her in coarse and sexually suggestive

Afrikaans, so they were mortified when Margie and Trev thanked them in their own language for the ride to shore.

Chapter 8

Cape Town, South Africa

22 December 1975 - 20 February 1976

After clearing South African Customs, we berthed *Dolphin* at the Cape Royal Yacht Club. Margie phoned her parents who came down to the dock and welcomed us enthusiastically. Margie's mother Desirée asked what we'd like for our first meal on shore. We all requested bacon and eggs with fresh bread and butter. Margie's dad Louis sped to a near-by bakery, returning with still-warm rolls that were a real treat after more than a month at sea.

My first priority was to deliver Her Majesty's mail from Tristan da Cunha to the Cape Town postmaster. This was a hassle since he was out to lunch when I arrived at the main post office, and I had to wait a long time to see him. Then, before the mail could be accepted, I had to fill out an archaic form listing details about me, my boat, my crew, our voyage ("Number of births during last leg of voyage, Number of deaths," etc.). The postmaster thanked me for my service and told me *Dolphin*'s passage time of twelve days had been quite fast for the time of year.

Dolphin stayed in Cape Town for the next two months. I knew my WGI business needed my immediate supervision, so I flew back to California two days after our arrival. The yacht club official requested that we move *Dolphin* to a long-term berth in an outer marina. It seemed a little isolated to me, so as a security measure, Alfie stayed on board full time for several days while Margie and Trev went to stay with her parents. They went food shopping first, so Alfie would have fresh food, fruit juice, and coffee. Unfortunately, they all forgot to buy eggs. "Eggs are very important," said Alfie. Margie directed him to the yacht club convenience store and gave him some South African money. She and Trev then went off to stay at her parents' home. Alfie reported later that he walked fifteen minutes to the store to buy a half dozen eggs. The shop assistant asked him something in English and he decided to say "Yes," without understanding the question. After a fifteen-minute walk back to *Dolphin*, he readied the frying pan with a blob of sizzling butter, poised the egg to crack into the pan, and tapped and tapped—the egg was hard-boiled, and Alfie almost cried!

While I was in California, Margie wrote me that she and Trev took Alfie to her parents' home for a few nights to celebrate Christmas together. They spent their holidays lazing in the gardens around the pool and taking in the magnificent view of the Blue Mountains in the distance. Alfie brought the swim fins along from *Dolphin*. He put on the "*grande* shoes," and jumped into the deep end. He emerged sputtering and gasping, "¡*Ayúdame, Margarita*!" ("Help me, Margarita!") It turned out that he couldn't swim a stroke! On Chilean fishing boats, a fisherman who fell into the water was left to drown, and Alfie had never learned to swim. No wonder he hadn't been interested in swimming with us in the mid-Atlantic! He had done several very daring things, including climbing up the mast, without a life jacket. Now that I knew he couldn't swim, his inclination to steer *Dolphin* toward land became more understandable.

On my return from the U.S., I landed first in Johannesburg, and found myself amidst another bureaucratic hassle when the Customs agents found me with a "dirty" book. Réanne had given me a copy of Erica Jong's best-seller *Fear of Flying* to read on the plane. It was considered a pornographic book at the time and banned in apartheid-era South Africa. My copy was confiscated as soon as I landed in Johannesburg. I was annoyed, because I hadn't finished reading it, and I made a lot of noise about the violation of my rights as an American citizen. The officials at the Johannesburg airport insisted that I would have to fly on to Cape Town without the book. I remembered a bit of a maritime law stating that an American vessel flying a U.S. flag was considered to be American territory. I called the office of the U.S. Ambassador in South Africa, and told them I was the Captain of an American vessel and that my rights were being violated. The office called the airport officials and demanded they return my book. They agreed to do this, but only after they'd marked it with special ink so if it were found anywhere but on my boat, I'd be arrested and sentenced to eight years at hard labor in a South African jail. Petty bureaucracy has always rubbed me the wrong way, and I've always stood up for my rights, even for relatively trivial issues.

Once back in Cape Town, I heard that a woman mariner, Ann Gash, was due to arrive after sailing single-handed across the Indian Ocean from her hometown near Sydney, Australia. Local newspapers had reported extensively on her amazing voyage. She had learned to sail in her forties, and after her six children were grown, she decided to take a trip from southeast Australia to England in her 26-foot plywood Folkboat, *Ilimo*. She told her family she was going to spend time sailing along the Australian coast, but she neglected to mention her ultimate destination. Her family only realized her plans when she sent them a letter from Christmas Island, off the coast of Java, several months and thousands of miles into her voyage.

I greeted Ann at the dock when she arrived, and she and I connected immediately as fellow veterans of the self-inflicted ordeal of small sailboat voyaging. Ann's passage to Cape Town had been arduous and lonely, and she was desperate for human companionship. We spent several days together on her boat, and I held her in my arms for hours as she decompressed from the rigors of her trip. After she had recovered, we went on hikes through the aromatic *fynbos* (South African brush) around Cape Town, which reminded me of the chaparral of my Southern California home. Ann eventually wrote a book about her trip, *And a Star to Steer Her By*. I still treasure the letters she sent me from various ports as she continued her voyage.

I enjoyed my time in Cape Town, but I was eager to get *Dolphin* back to sea where she and I belonged. One afternoon, I took some South African friends out for a day sail. My biggest U.S. flag streamed behind as we deliberately passed very close to Robben Island, where Mandela was imprisoned. I vividly imagined sailing in close enough to the prison that he might see us and swim to freedom. Of course he didn't, but I still hoped that he had seen our flag and recognized it as a sign of support, however indirect. In reality, of course, Mandela had his own long-term plan that was better for both him and his country.

I had another glimpse of the rottenness of apartheid-era South Africa when I went into a Cape Town bank. Banks were one of the few places in the city that weren't segregated. The bank I entered was full of people of all colors waiting in long lines for service. As always, I was impatient and thought I saw a gap in one line that was close to the front. In my hurry to move, I accidentally knocked down an elderly black man. I apologized repeatedly and tried to help him up, but he cowered before me. "No master, my fault, my fault." This was bullshit; it hadn't been his fault at all; it was mine. This incident bothered me for a long time afterwards, and I decided that the fault lay with the apartheid system—a form of government so evil that it overruled reality.

After my few days with Ann Gash, I spent my free time with Judy. She was a friend of Margie's family and the widow of one of Dr. Christiaan Barnard's early heart transplant patients. Judy and I vacationed together at a cabin on the Indian Ocean side of the Cape of Good Hope. The water looked inviting and I went for a swim, but I wasn't used to the unique curl of the waves—a tight snap-and-roll motion that caught me by surprise and dumped me on the bottom, dislocating my shoulder. I was in ten feet of water and several hundred yards offshore. With my good arm I tried waving to Judy, but she didn't realize I was in trouble and merely waved back. My dislocated shoulder was floating up behind my head and there was no way I could swim. The only thing I could do was to sink to the bottom, flex my knees, and force myself up and forward through the water. I did this countless times, grabbing breaths whenever I broke the surface and making a foot or two of headway each time. Eventually I got close enough to shore that Judy could see I was in trouble. She helped me get to the beach and then into her Mercedes (where, like a lot of wealthy, white South Africans, she kept a pistol). She drove me to the Cape Town hospital where her late husband had undergone his surgery. She knew all of the staff, but not my last name when they filled out the paperwork for my treatment, which was a slight embarrassment.

My shoulder was restored to its proper place, and I was discharged with instructions not to raise my elbow higher than my waist for a couple of weeks. Of course, I forgot all about this when I got back to Judy's house. While she went out to refill her car with gas (which was strictly rationed so she was always afraid of running out), I lay on the floor and assumed my favorite resting position with my hands behind my head. Out popped the shoulder. I waited in agony for Judy to return, and then she drove me straight back to the hospital. In the meantime, my muscles had tightened up. I was given extra morphine and it took the same two doctors who had treated me earlier and were still on duty, pulling and pushing against me with all their strength, bouncing me up and down on the gurney, to put my shoulder right a second time. The doctors repeated their instructions about not raising my arm, and this time I listened!

Judy worked as head clerk for a Cape Town bank, which at that time was the highest position a woman could attain in banking in South Africa. I was sure she'd have more career opportunities if she emigrated to the U.S., and I phoned Réanne in California to ask if Judy could live with us until she got a job. Réanne had agreed that she and I would have an open marriage for the duration of our separation. However, Réanne objected to letting Judy live with us in California and asked the principal at her school if she could have a couple of weeks off to visit me in South Africa and deal with what she thought was a bona fide marital crisis. Her principal was sympathetic and agreed she could go, while I reported back to Judy that Réanne wasn't too pleased about my idea. Judy, in turn, wasn't too happy with Réanne's response, but I told her that Réanne was my wife and her wishes would always come first. Judy got snooty with me and didn't have any sympathy for Réanne's position, so I called Réanne back and told her I'd changed my mind about Judy. This reassured Réanne enough that she no longer felt the need to fly to Cape Town.

*   *   *   *   *

I began to plan the next leg of my circumnavigation. *Dolphin* was already halfway around the world, and my three crewmembers were eager to accompany me onward. I examined the cracked main mast, but I didn't think that the damage would prevent continuing our journey. The rest of the boat systems were in fine shape, although the bilges still needed pumping every day. I knew more frequent pumping would be necessary while crossing the turbulent Indian Ocean.

Other factors were working against me. All the way across the Atlantic, I had hoped Réanne would rejoin us while we continued our eastward passage. However, while I was in California, Réanne told me about a friend sailing a small boat across the Indian Ocean that summer who was feared lost at sea. This was enough to spook Réanne, who told me decisively she would not to come back to finish the trip. Once I knew Réanne wouldn't come back to finish the circumnavigation, I hadn't been able to persuade any other lady sailors to accompany me the rest of the way around the world.

In addition, in spite of my recent trip home, increasing problems with WGI were starting to require my focused attention back in California, and I realized that I had to deal with them sooner rather than later. Mundane business concerns were pursuing me around the globe, thwarting my desire to live freely on the open ocean. It was clear that I needed to break off the trip and head for home. If I had to reenter the world of working stiffs, the fastest sailing route to California would be westward, back across the Atlantic, through the Panama Canal, and up the west coast of Mexico. With profound regret, I decided to cut short my dream and head west.

My three crewmembers were agreeable to the change in plan, Trev in particular. He had extensive experience as a stage designer in Cape Town, and he had a strong desire to work in Hollywood. Margie and Alfie were also eager to go to California.

Trev and Margie in Cape Town

* * * * *

Trev and Margie decided to get married before we left on the first leg of the return journey. The wedding was held two days before our scheduled departure in her parent's garden, so there was quite a flurry of preparation. Trev's two daughters were flower girls, and I was the best man. I took advantage of the opportunity to give Margie a congratulatory kiss. It was the only kiss I gave her on the entire voyage! We enjoyed a magnificent wedding banquet complete with lovely flowers and lots of great South African wines. The party went on late into the night, and there were some sore heads in the morning as the crew raced around to finish provisioning *Dolphin*. We bought fresh fruits and vegetables, salad ingredients, fresh meat for a couple of days, and baked treats like biscuits and cakes. We had already replenished the dried and canned goods. Our next certain destination would be Trinidad, in the eastern Caribbean off the coast of Venezuela—a passage that would take at least 45 days. I hoped to stop for a day or two at the island of St. Helena en route so I could replenish the water and diesel, but I feared being too dependent on shore supplies after the difficulties we'd experienced in trying to land at Tristan.

My shoulder was better and we were almost ready to set sail when a young American man on crutches turned up at the dock and asked if he could come with us. Bob's legs were stunted from childhood polio, but his upper body was strong and healthy, and he thought he'd be capable of working on a sailboat since he could use the handholds and rigging to move around. Bob had been stranded in South Africa after spending several months on a religious retreat, and he was looking for a ride back to the U.S. I was reluctant to take him along since I didn't expect him to be much use, but he was persistent, and the rest of the crew argued in his favor, making the case that we could use his money to buy extra food and booze for the voyage. Bob committed to work under my orders so I agreed to take him along for the cost of an airplane ticket to the States, and he joined our crew as we set out to recross the Atlantic.

Bob steering Dolphin away from Cape Town. Note the cloud "table cloth" covering Table Mountain.

Chapter 9

Cape Town, South Africa to Saint Helena

21 February - 6 March, 1976

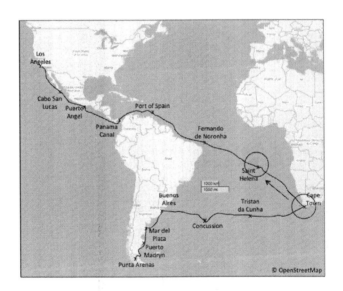

Departure is my favorite part of any voyage, when I anticipate all of the adventures and unknowns ahead. Margie and Trev's friends and families gave us a great send-off, crowding onto *Dolphin* for a few last words. Margie's father Louis was late and had not yet appeared by the time we were ready to leave. We could only wait another few minutes before we lost the tide, and eventually we had to leave without his goodbye. Margie was pretty upset! We cast off all the lines, and then in the distance I could see Louis running along the jetty. I motored back and pulled alongside the jetty, just long enough for Margie to hop off for a goodbye hug.

Before we departed Cape Town, I made it clear to Bob, as I had to the others, that if he brought any drugs aboard—"I mean anything, from aspirin on up"—I would kill him, throw his body overboard, and tell the officials at the next port that he'd disappeared during a night watch. This was no idle threat. If Customs officers found anything illicit on board, my crew would get shipped home but I would lose my boat. I never did have to throw anybody overboard, but as captain I had a lot of power— more than most people ever experience on land. Boats are worlds unto themselves, and I was the supreme authority. I saw myself less as Captain Bligh than Captain Cook, however. Cook was more than just a great navigator and explorer. He was a rational man of science who had enlightened ideas about things like keeping his crew as healthy as possible.

Our new crewmember, Bob, was in his mid-twenties, and from Michigan. He seemed eager to learn and fit in, and he had a quiet and pleasant personality. He got around on *Dolphin* pretty well in spite of needing arm-crutches when he was on land. Leaving the harbor for the open ocean thrilled him, and he had trouble containing his excitement although like a lot of new sailors, he also had trouble containing his stomach. The ride out of Cape Town was bumpy in the big troughs. We put up full sails, and *Dolphin* treated us to a slow downward roll and a fast upward lift over the tops of the swells. Margie prepared a nice dinner of roast beef that no one could eat, and Alfie and Bob were physically sick.

Dolphin was in the main shipping lane the next morning, so we had quite a few ships for company, including fishing trawlers as well as huge cargo and container ships, tankers, and naval vessels. Although large ships supposedly have radar and crews standing watch, smaller boats are regularly run down and sunk without the larger ships ever being aware of their presence. That same morning, we sighted a whale as big as *Dolphin*. We kept an eye out in case the creature decided to get too close, since whales have been known to approach sailboats with possibly amorous intent. I was still sure that a whale had struck *Dolphin* on our way to Tristan da Cunha, and I didn't want a repeat performance. We were also accompanied by dolphins for a long stretch, and we saw a few small albatrosses. Bob was surprised to find so much activity in the vast ocean.

At nightfall, we were treated to a brilliant starry sky. Orion's familiar belt pointed due south toward the Southern Cross. The constellation of Aquarius was easy to pick out. Phosphorescence streamed from the dolphins as they played alongside in the dark sea, almost like a reflection of the brilliant stars overhead.

As we sailed northward across latitude 30°S, the wind dropped. An intermittent breeze rose and fell, and the helmsman had to concentrate hard to keep the boat sailing well. The wind eventually increased as rain started, and gusts to Force 6 produced a short chop on top of the huge ocean swells. Befitting her name, *Dolphin* rolled exuberantly, and we all had to struggle to keep our balance. Our speed averaged seven knots since my noon shot, and several times we surfed along as fast as ten knots. Seawater washed over the decks with an entire bucketful slopping into the cabin through the upper aft porthole. While trying to photograph a wave off the stern quarter, I got completely "pooped", and had to change my clothes and take apart the camera to dry it. The water temperature was an almost pleasant 70 °F, unlike our first entrance to the Atlantic from the Strait of Magellan. We dropped the twin jib at nightfall for peace of mind. The next morning, Bob reported a tear in the mainsail, so we raised the twin jib again to take some pressure off.

We had a great day overall as *Dolphin* roared along, surfing the ten foot swells. That night, Bob had a terrible nightmare, waking the sleeping crew. He screamed, yelled, kicked, and fell out of his bunk. Maybe the unfamiliar movement of the boat disoriented him, but I worried that he was possibly having drug withdrawal symptoms. We woke him up, and he calmed down and went back to sleep. After being awakened by the uproar, Margie got up and sat with Alfie on the late watch. They decided to lower the twin jib to reduce our speed and heeling. I went above to see what had changed the boat's motion. They'd made a good decision since the reduced sail kept *Dolphin* on a more even keel while we continued to make seven knots. It was much more comfortable for everyone, and another indication of the crew's development as blue-water sailors. Warm seas and warm weather combined to make this a very enjoyable trip. The next day, I finished reading *Fear of Flying* and spent some time thinking about the changing roles that women had experienced in my lifetime.

The volume of vessel traffic surprised me after our relatively lonely crossing from Argentina to South Africa. The 1,000-foot-long supertanker *World Happiness* passed northbound within a half-mile of us, powering along at twenty knots. It was a sobering sight since even with their radar and watch standers *Dolphin* would have been almost invisible to them at night. That evening, Alfie fell asleep during his helm watch. Margie had been wakeful again and went up to chat with him around 0130 hours. She got the shock of her life when she saw a huge ship with lights blazing quickly bearing down on *Dolphin* from astern. She hollered for me, and I turned on the spotlight to illuminate the sails from high up on the mast. The ship was within 200 yards of us and not deviating from her course. The autopilot must have been running everything. We had no alternative but to tack instantly and change course abruptly. The huge bow wave threw the boat around, tossing Trev right out of his bunk. I was furious with Alfie since a collision would have cost our lives.

Nobody went back to sleep that night, and the next morning we were all pretty grumpy. Alfie was deeply ashamed of himself and very gloomy, and the rest of the crew was suffering from lack of sleep. Margie had a case of homesickness mixed with some post-wedding blues. She talked about jumping ship in St. Helena and returning to South Africa. I cheered everyone up by pulling out a watermelon I had hidden in the bilges. Margie's mood also improved when I told her I would help her and Trev find work in California, and that afternoon I managed to contact a ham radio operator in Johannesburg who relayed our position to Margie's family.

Bob repinning the jib poles.

Alfie remained unlike himself and stayed extremely glum and withdrawn. He felt his failure on watch very deeply. Margie tried to cheer him up, but he brooded all day. She found some tomatoes that were still green when we left Cape Town, and cooked a Malaysian dish called Tomato Bredie, with lamb and lots of vegetables. Everyone else enjoyed it, but Alfie was still too upset to eat much.

Happily for the overall mood, the following day Alfie had a chance to redeem himself and feel good about life again. The port jib pole fell when the pin pulled out, and the pole swung wildly at the clew of the jib. We dropped the jib and stowed the pole. In the process, Alfie accidently dropped the main halyard, which shot all the way up to the top of the mast. He grabbed the steel shrouds and climbed up hand over hand to recover the halyard. It was a dangerous thing to do since he was swinging through the air like a pendulum and not wearing a life jacket, but he managed to grab the halyard. When he got down, I sent Bob up on the boson's chair to pin the wires down. It was a team effort, but Alfie's mood changed dramatically and he was happy to have done something constructive.

The dolphins returned, and we began encountering flying fish, a sign that we were reaching the doldrums. I dreaded the slow tropical days rolling from side to side on a boat that was hardly moving forward. By February 28, we were all but becalmed and we had to start the motor again. Still, Dolphin had made 1,026 miles in the seven days from Cape Town, a new record run for a week's travel. The water and air were both a pleasant 75 °F. The upside of being stuck in the tropics was that we had time to repair sails, perform other maintenance work, and clean up. We scrubbed the decks and did housekeeping chores below. I bled the various filters, checked the oil and water, lubricated the head, and took the saltwater galley pump apart to replace the diaphragms. The pump had been leaking salt water on the floor since Cape Town. We also had time to suntan, read, swim, and even shower with a small ration of fresh water. Using a spare halyard, we raised a plastic canister up into the rigging for the afternoon and let the sun warm the water. Margie took the first short shower, and then the rest of us followed. It was a challenge to apply soap and rinse quickly while the stream of water remained. Often the last person would have to rinse with salt water.

I tried some radio contacts. Bob spoke with someone in New Jersey, but I was disappointed when I couldn't get through to Réanne. The lack of wind kept us motoring through the night and next day. Trev called me at 0100 to witness a weird sight. He'd noticed a strong fishy odor, and turned on the spotlight. The sea was choked with wriggling worms the size of rice grains. After a few minutes the smell—and the worms—disappeared behind us. In the morning the seas and winds continued calm, and the sun was hidden by high clouds. Schools of flying fish erupted out of the water in front of the bow and skimmed away for two to three hundred feet. At first, they sounded like raindrops hitting the water, and then twenty or thirty fish of about six to eight inches long would fly off over the surface. Sometimes their tails dragged behind them, so they resembled a flock of small taxiing airplanes. Were they generating speed by moving their tails? How did they know which way the wind was blowing while they were still underwater?

Margie worked hard to keep the meals interesting and healthy. Breakfast was usually canned fruit (mostly grapefruit), corn flakes with powdered milk, cheese and bacon omelets, and whole wheat crackers. One day we had canned salmon with mayo, tomato, pickle and mixed bean salad, asparagus and beets with relish and cheese, crackers and pineapple for lunch. Dinner was corned beef fritters, roasted potatoes, Brussels sprouts with mushrooms, sweet carrots, and canned guavas with cream. No one complained about her menus although Bob had developed some sores in his mouth that made eating acid foods very painful.

Several times we sighted sharks, sometimes swimming within fifty yards of us. But with or without sharks underneath us, the heat of the days was so intense that cooling dips were in order. With Bob accompanying him and securely tied to a safety line, Alfie took his first-ever dip off the boat, wearing the "*grande shoes*" and a life jacket. Trev was on duty to pull him in rapidly if a shark was sighted. Margie and I were stronger swimmers, and ventured farther from the boat. Trev never risked a swim and always placed himself on "shark patrol" with my .22 rifle.

As we sailed northward and the weather got warmer, Bob continued to suffer terrible nightmares every night. We couldn't help him, and he disturbed everyone's rest. The sores in his mouth worsened, and he developed a hideous rash on his arms and legs which opened up into huge discharging sores. I became more suspicious that he was recovering from a drug habit, and I instructed Margie to conceal the morphine from our medical kit deep inside her backpack, although Trev and Alfie knew where it was in case of emergency. After talking to Bob about his condition, I found out he'd been on a religious retreat somewhere in the African bush and had subsisted almost entirely on peanut butter and gruel for three months. In spite of Margie's meals, Bob was suffering from gross vitamin deficiency. In other words—and in spite of my respect for Captain Cook—I had old-fashioned scurvy aboard my boat!

Scurvy, which is caused by a deficiency of Vitamin C (ascorbic acid), used to be common among sailors who spent months at sea eating little more than salt pork and hard tack. Even if scurvy failed to kill them directly, it caused teeth to fall out as well as skin lesions and fever. The weakness and lethargy that were also symptoms of the disease contributed to many shipwrecks. Scurvy was a major problem for European navies and explorers from the age of Columbus onwards. Many aboriginal societies had herbal remedies for scurvy, and a Scottish naval surgeon, James Lind, advocated the eating of citrus fruits as a treatment in his book of 1753, *A Treatise on Scurvy.* The Royal Navy ignored Lind's advice for several decades, but all British ships were eventually required to carry supplies of lime juice, which is the reason British sailors are sometimes called "limeys." Vitamin C is necessary in humans for the synthesis of collagen, a protein in bones and other tissues, and it can be found in almost all fruits in addition to citrus, and in most green vegetables. This was not known scientifically until 1932, but back in the 18th century Captain Cook believed that sauerkraut might work as a more practical dietary supplement for long sea voyages than Lind's citrus fruits. Cook famously circumnavigated the world from 1768-1771 with barrels of the stuff, and without losing a single man to scurvy. In fact, sauerkraut has relatively low levels of Vitamin C, but Cook also practiced exceptional shipboard hygiene and made sure to take on fresh food supplies at every opportunity.

Scurvy still occurs in parts of the world where malnutrition is endemic, and occasionally in First World countries when people ignore nutritional advice. And now I had it aboard *Dolphin*! Bob's case had not progressed much beyond boils and mouth sores, but the boils were gross. He treated them by rinsing them in seawater and applying disinfectant lotion beneath gauze dressings that had to be changed several times a day. The medical kit contained a box of a thousand four-inch-square gauze dressings. I had previously thought that *Dolphin* was well prepared for medical emergencies, but Bob eventually used up the entire supply of gauze bandages. It was clear he needed to see a doctor, both to confirm my diagnosis and to receive whatever treatment was required. In the meantime, I suffered almost as much as Bob from the sheer ignominy of having a scurvy crewman.

By Tuesday, March 2, *Dolphin* was 400 nautical miles from St. Helena. We motored all night in calm seas and winds. By morning we had Force 1-2 winds and put up all the sails. Margie hard-boiled all of the remaining eggs as they were getting a little past their prime. Off watch, Trev spent his time under the sunshade in the cockpit reading Jules Verne. Margie read in her bunk, and I finished Edward Abbey's *Desert Solitaire*. We were a harmonious group in the peaceful surroundings.

The next night we motored again. I was able to get a radio contact for Margie to chat with her family, which cheered her up. The sky clouded and rain squalls started to move in. At 0415 hours, Alfie woke me when he noticed a strange light in the distance. It looked like a single blinking light on a ship that was approaching quickly from astern. After observing it for several minutes, I determined that it was either a bright star or a plane low on the horizon. The light was apparently blinking as distant swells momentarily obscured it. It was a peculiar effect, and I praised Alfie for wakening me after our previous near miss.

For the next several days, the weather continued calm with the usual southern swells. During daylight hours, we kept all the sails up in hopes of catching any light breezes, but it was the engine that kept us moving closer to St. Helena. The air temperature was now 85°F, and the water was 75°F. We enjoyed swim breaks and smooth motoring in the light airs. I finally managed to get a radio contact through to Réanne, who said she would meet me in Trinidad—yippee! Maybe I had to cut my dream short, but at least Réanne would be sharing part of the journey, and I was sure she'd enjoy sailing in the Caribbean much more than in the extreme conditions near Cape Horn.

At about 1100 hours on March 6, we spotted land ahead on the port bow. This was St. Helena, a volcanic island similar to Tristan da Cunha, although with a much more humid and tropical climate since it lies at a latitude of only 15°S, compared to Tristan's 37°S. St. Helena is a British possession and the administrative center for Tristan da Cunha and Ascensión Island as well. The capital of Jamestown lies on the northwest side of the island, so we had to sail almost halfway around St. Helena before arriving in port.

The shore looked formidable with stark brown lava cliffs pockmarked with caves. Just as at Tristan and Punta Arenas, the "port" is an open roadstead with no sheltered place to tie up or anchor. However, the wind and swells were much more accommodating than they had been for us at Tristan. Two other yachts, *Kantread* and *Caprice,* were already tied up to an old mooring buoy. There were also a couple of dozen longboats that clearly belonged to the island. *Kantread*, was a thirty foot Giles design. Her skipper, Pierre, rowed out to meet us and invited us to share the mooring. *Caprice* was a twenty-eight foot sloop from New Zealand that had arrived just two hours before us. The young couple aboard her had been cruising since their four-month-old baby had been born, and they were planning to continue on around the world. *Dolphin* was bigger than either of the other boats, but both were sturdy ocean-going yachts, well embarked on circumnavigations.

It was 1900 hours and pitch dark by the time we moored. Someone on shore had seen us arrive however, and forty-five minutes later three officials appeared alongside in a rowboat. They were the port captain, a Mr. Richards, along with a medical officer and an unarmed policeman who did double duty as the island's immigration officer. We filled out the required paperwork, a simple form with no associated fee. The medical officer accepted my word that we had all been vaccinated for smallpox and said there was a doctor on shore who could examine Bob. Their official duties done, the men each accepted a glass of brandy and told us about St. Helena.

At about fifty square miles, the island of St. Helena is almost one and a half times the size of Tristan da Cunha. The most recent volcanic eruption occurred more than seven million years ago, versus Tristan's eruption of 1961. The millions of years of erosion have lowered the summit of the main volcano to 2,684 feet, compared to Tristan's 6,765 feet, which explained why we could see Tristan from so much farther out to sea. At the time of our visit, St. Helena had approximately 5,000 residents living in several settlements including the capital of Jamestown, which had about 1,500 people. There was neither phone nor television service on the island then, nor did it have an airport. A supply ship (RMS *St. Helena*) made just a couple of scheduled stops a year on its run between Southampton and Cape Town. The only other visitors came from transiting yachts, of which *Dolphin* was the seventeenth that summer. A twice-monthly boat service operated between St. Helena and Ascensión Island, about 800 miles to the northwest. Unlike Tristan, with its lucrative rock lobster exports, St. Helena had no current major source of export earnings at the time of our visit. Nowadays, the island is a popular destination for recreational divers since the historic shipwrecks provide excellent opportunities to dive in the clear tropical waters.

The policeman told me there were no guns on the island, and the Jamestown jail held no prisoners. But people did go stir crazy sometimes. Three years earlier, a couple of boys had stolen a visiting yacht while her crew of six was at the hotel sleeping off a bender. The boys headed for Brazil but ran out of water after a few days and had only beer to drink. They were eventually rescued by the Brazilian Navy.

St. Helena also had its share of shipwrecks. Mr. Richards said that in the morning we would be able to see the protruding mast of the steamer *Papanui*, which sank close to shore in 1911 after the coal in its bunkers caught fire; the 364 passengers and crew were saved and cared for by the islanders. The submerged wreck of a supply ship, the *Darkdale* lay further out, sunk in 1944 by a German submarine. St. Helena had hazards ashore as well. Jamestown is wedged into a cleft between two unstable lava flows. In 1890, a 1500-ton rock fall had killed nine people. "But by all means, go ashore," Mr. Richards said. He told us where we could obtain supplies, and said we should make a point of climbing Jacob's Ladder, a 699-step staircase leading up to an old British fort at the top of the hill behind the town. The steps were a replacement for a cableway built in 1829 to lift supplies from the port of Jamestown up to Ladder Hill Fort high abovethe town, and were now one of the must-see attractions of Saint Helena.

After completing immigration control, we ate dinner and headed for town by dinghy. We tied up at the rickety little jetty, and strolled down the main street to the hotel. We sat outside on the verandah in the balmy night air enjoying ice cold beers and chatting to the islanders and the Frenchmen from *Kantread*.

St. Helena has been a British possession since 1673, when the English East India Company took formal possession of the island and built a fort to protect South Atlantic and Indian trade routes. The opening of the Suez Canal in 1869 reduced St. Helena's fortunes, as the island lost some of its strategic significance. St. Helena is most famous nowadays as the place where Napoleon Bonaparte served his second exile, after the final defeat of his army by the British and their allies at the Battle of Waterloo in June of 1815. Napoleon's first exile was to the small Mediterranean island of Elba the previous year, after he failed to conquer Russia and was forced to abdicate as Emperor of France. The famous palindrome, or sentence that reads the same forwards and backwards, *Able was I ere I saw Elba,* is based on Napoleon's first exile. He escaped from Elba in February 1815, but his conquest of Europe finally ended in defeat at Waterloo in Belgium four months later. Although he might have fled to the United States, the British blocked his escape, and he surrendered to them on July 15, 1815.

Napoleon arrived on St. Helena three months later with an entourage of twenty-seven. The residents of the island were given only a few days' notice that they were coming, and to deter any French rescue attempts, the British established military garrisons on Tristan da Cunha and Ascensión Islands, as well as St. Helena. The ex-Emperor was housed in a damp, dilapidated mansion, Longwood House, and died there six years later in 1821 at the age of 51. He supposedly died of stomach cancer although it's easy to imagine that boredom may have played a role. Napoleon was buried on the island. His tomb is located in a beautiful valley near the house although his body was repatriated to France in 1840. In 1858, his original gravesite and Longwood House were given as property to the French.

Early the following morning, Alfie and I quietly rowed ashore and brought freshly baked rolls, piping hot croissants and a big jug of hot coffee back to the boat for breakfast—a welcome surprise for the rest of the crew. After breakfast, we all went ashore to buy supplies for the next leg of *Dolphin*'s voyage. I also had to make sure that Bob was properly diagnosed and treated, and Alfie needed to find a dentist.

Enormous dark lava flows loomed over Jamestown, which was crammed into a narrow valley. The cobbled streets and stone buildings felt quite constricted. As we set out on our various errands, we met up with the other cruisers: the two French men from *Kantread* and the New Zealand couple with their baby. We decided to rent a pick-up truck together to explore the island. Our first stop was Napoleon's mansion and the site of his first tomb. The house where he had lived and died in exile had been turned into a museum and was painted a surprising shade of pink. We spent an hour wandering around enjoying the French décor and antique furniture. Then we drove to the bottom of the long, steep stairs of "Jacob's Ladder." The Frenchmen ran right up to the top. Alfie and Margie went halfway up with them, stopping when they got too winded, and then joined them on their way back down. I waited with Bob and Trev at the base, chatting and enjoying the view, while Trev had a smoke.

The glorious tropical vegetation satisfied our hunger for bright color and fresh fragrance after the long time at sea. Lush frangipane and bougainvillea draped walls and scented the air. On our trip around Jamestown, we saw two giant tortoises on the lawn outside Plantation House—the official residence of the Governor of the British Overseas Territories in the South Atlantic. The tortoises were both huge and ancient, at over 500 pounds and well over one hundred years old. During the 17th century, giant tortoises were an important commodity. Hundreds at a time were taken from islands in the Indian Ocean and stacked in the holds of ships, almost like containers, to be used for emergency rations. When we visited, the oldest tortoise on St. Helena was called Jonathan. According to a recent BBC report, he

St. Helena's harbor from Jacob's Ladder with *Dolphin* visible at the top.

is still there, and is now reputed to be the world's oldest living animal. He is thought to have arrived on St. Helena in 1882 after hatching in the Seychelles in 1832.

While strolling around the quaint streets, I noticed two beautiful women, possibly mother and daughter, leaning on a blue wooden Dutch door at the entrance to their white-washed home. They were standing happily in the early morning sunshine watching the passers-by. They were exotic, mocha colored, mixed-race women with large brown eyes. Their brightly colored silk dresses were piped with white lace and extremely becoming. I stopped for a brief chat and we all exchanged a laugh when I complimented them on their attire.

We cruisers all met up again that evening for a meal at the hotel. It was expensive and not the greatest food, but the company was enjoyable. The animated conversation was a welcome change after spending so many days confined aboard our small boat with the same crew.

The next morning, we set out to finish our land errands so we could depart that afternoon. As we hustled up the street, an old, crippled man met us on the dock brandishing what looked like a small, flat brandy bottle. "Souvenir! Souvenir!" he cried. I wasn't interested since I was in a hurry to pick up our passports at the police station and to get Bob to the only doctor in town. Trev and Margie looked more closely at what was in the bottle. It was a perfect model of *Dolphin,* sails and all, with a picture of St. Helena as a backdrop. The old guy had obviously studied the boat in the moonlight and worked all night on the model. Trev and Margie bought it on the spot. They presented it to Réanne and me at the conclusion of our voyage and I still keep it on my desk today.

The sole doctor in Jamestown saw Bob and confirmed my diagnosis of scurvy. I would have put him ashore and left him there, but the doctor told me that there wasn't enough Vitamin C on the whole island to treat him. The doctor gave me half of the one large bottle which was the island's entire supply, and told me that ethically, he needed to keep the rest of it for other emergencies. He lanced some of the boils, and gave Bob a treatment plan. Meanwhile, Alfie had two teeth pulled, so he didn't feel too well either.

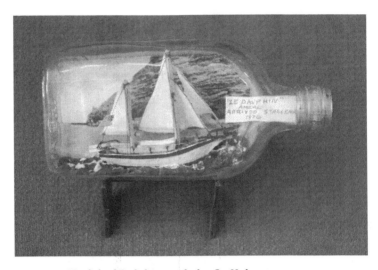

Model of *Dolphin* made by St. Helena man

Before departing St. Helena, we pumped fifty-seven gallons of diesel into the fuel tank, and lashed two additional fuel drums onto the foredeck. I didn't want to miss Réanne in Trinidad for lack of wind! We also topped off all of the available water containers so that *Dolphin* was carrying 150 gallons. There was no fresh produce available, since we'd missed the weekly market day, but Margie had managed to purchase a dozen loaves of double-baked bread, a stalk of bananas, a case of wine, two dozen eggs, candy, and some more fishhooks. I picked up our passports at the police station. The port captain had our departure clearance in an envelope already stamped by Customs, but required £2.15 for port fees for our thirty-six hour stay. St. Helena had been a charming break in the middle of our long Atlantic crossing, but Trinidad beckoned, and we were off!

Chapter 10

Saint Helena to Port of Spain, Trinidad

6 March, 1976 - 7 April, 1976

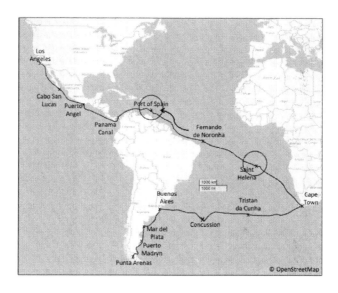

The distance from St. Helena to our next stop in Trinidad was 3,800 miles, comparable to the 3,900 miles from Buenos Aires to Cape Town. That earlier crossing had taken thirty-two days, but we'd had the benefits of favorable currents and winds. Our westward crossing would take longer, since the currents and winds were counter to our course, and I estimated that *Dolphin* would need thirty to forty days to reach the Caribbean Sea. I stressed how conservative we needed to be with our fresh water. With just 150 gallons of water and five people aboard, I limited each person's usage to one quart per day for the passage. This was not much water for the tropics, but I needed to ensure that *Dolphin* had a reserve in case of accident or delay.

We motored for the first several days, as there was no wind to speak of. Catching a good-sized yellow-fin tuna provided some excitement on the second day. Margie prepared it with fresh salad and French fries for lunch. Alfie was still suffering from having two molars pulled and skipped the tuna, but he was able to eat an egg and some fish roe. We dined under the shade cloth in the cockpit, while *Dolphin* imitated a motorboat, churning along in the mid-Atlantic Ocean.

During a good hard rainsquall the next morning, we captured as much fresh water as we could in buckets and pans. Everyone appreciated having a whole bucket to use at his or her own discretion.

By the third day, we had picked up some speed, sailing smoothly with Force 3 winds. I was still testing different variations of rigging *Dolphin*'s sails, and I got great results from running the mizzen staysail sheet through the genoa track. We experienced some rolling in the long Atlantic swells, and several times waves drenched Trev and Margie's bunk through an open hatch, as well as soaking some cockpit cushions and navigational equipment. A large school of dorado, or dolphin fish, with their beautiful silver, gold, and pink colors surrounded us, filling the transparent sea. Streamlined and elegant, they looked like brilliant torpedoes darting along. That night a slight breeze kept us moving under clear skies and bright stars. The balmy weather encouraged us to enjoy a cocktail hour. Trev, Bob, and I sipped whisky, and Margie had vodka and orange. Alfie tried the vodka and got quite silly.

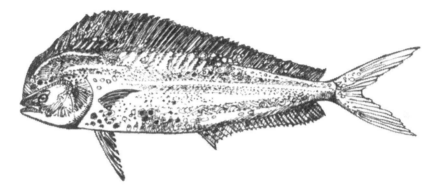

Even though we were moving right along, it didn't feel like it. *Dolphin*'s apparently slow progress toward my responsibilities in California aggravated me, and the camaraderie on board fluctuated. I found everyone more cantankerous and disagreeable than on our last ocean crossing. The least criticism set Bob and Margie into sulky fits. Bob's presence on board, as a new and less capable crew member, had changed the interpersonal dynamics. Personality clashes increased after our stop in St. Helena, and everyone seemed a lot more irritable. Bob was still seasick and uncomfortable from all his skin eruptions, and he was negative in his interactions with me and everyone else. His sulks and silences were aggressive and he grumbled about the food, which hurt the sores in his mouth. He didn't seem to be enjoying the trip, and his continual nightmares disturbed us all. I worried that his bad attitude would rub off on the rest of the crew, causing them to work less efficiently and slowing our passage. I had to speak sharply to him to get him to respect my authority as captain and give me space at the helm and table, but I wasn't going to let this guy's bad attitude keep me from meeting Réanne in Trinidad.

Alfie was still recovering from his dental ordeal in St. Helena, but his usual helpful good nature returned as he began to feel better. He certainly wasn't lazy or afraid of hard work. He sewed sails, washed dishes, baked bread, caught and cooked fish, and even eased Margie's job by cooking the occasional lunch or dinner. When he didn't feel like communicating, he just kept to himself without brooding, which I appreciated. Margie sometimes had dark moods, pouting and retreating to the foredeck with a book, although she always fulfilled her responsibilities, preparing excellent meals and taking a day watch so the helmsmen could have longer rests. The obvious fact that she and Trev were newlyweds fueled my longing for Réanne.

Around 0530 hours on March 13, I sighted what I thought was a new star. The following night I saw it again, brighter than before. I placed a radio call through to friends who'd read about it in the paper. It had already been named Comet West, although I think Comet Douglass would have had a nicer ring to it—if only I'd reported it first!

Alfie showering on deck

The weather continued fair with Force 3-4 winds all day, but the heat grew intense with air like an oven. Although humid, it was not unbearable, especially with the sunshade over part of the deck. There was still some rolling, and Alfie lost his blanket overboard after hanging it to dry. The crew wanted to stop for a swim, but *Dolphin* was making such good progress that I didn't want to slow down. We all dipped buckets of saltwater and showered on deck. The general mood seemed to improve as we resettled into our routine.

Margie continued to prepare excellent meals, with menus like corned beef and potatoes, green beans and onions in white sauce, and fresh fruit. Despite the heat, the hard-working crew welcomed this solid fare. Margie also boosted morale by creating sweet treats that we all eagerly anticipated—she baked the rapidly browning bananas into a delicious loaf served with sour cream made by adding lemon juice to some canned cream. We all appreciated her efforts, and I was pleased that we didn't waste anything. Meanwhile, the calm conditions gave us time for reading. I finished the *Memoirs of Chief Red Fox*, and Margie was reading *Lust for Life*, Irving Stone's biography of Vincent van Gogh.

On March 14, Margie scalded her arm with boiling water in the galley when the boat took an unexpected lurch. She put zinc ointment on the burn and then bandaged it with sterile gauze. *Dolphin*'s medical kit was still amply stocked, although Bob's psychological state and worsening boils concerned me. My anxiety increased as I couldn't seem to get a telephone patch through to Réanne via the ham radio operator. She was obviously out in the evenings. What was she doing? How I missed her! It helped a little to reread all of her letters and telegrams, but they were no substitute for her presence in my arms.

The next day, the air temperatures rose to 94 °F. We had smooth seas, no wind, and a bright blue sky with not a cloud in sight. In spite of the beautiful weather, it was amazing how quickly one person's bad mood led to grumpiness and squabbling throughout the entire crew. If I criticized Margie for something I didn't like in the galley, she'd snap at Bob, who'd promptly pick a fight with me. Soon the whole boat would be bickering. I assigned everyone chores to stave off boredom and quarreling. I did some engine work myself, checking engine filters and fluid levels and greasing the sail hanks. The rest of the crew scrubbed and rinsed the ship fore and aft and did laundry. Someone found a bar of good soap, which made washing quite luxurious. We all had a quick swim to wash away the sweat, until Alfie dumped a bucket of garbage over the side, joking that he was chumming for sharks. *Dolphin*'s good fishing lure had been lost, so Bob tried to fabricate something out of a copper strap, but it didn't seem to be very effective.

I finally got a radio message from Réanne that she would arrive in Port of Spain, Trinidad, via New York City, on April 9. I gave her a shopping list that included film, my vaccination record, ten bars of yellow salt-water soap, and sundry other boat supplies. Hearing Réanne's voice excited me, and I eagerly anticipated our rendezvous in Trinidad.

Force 1-2 breezes would spring up for several hours and then die again, leaving the sails limp and increasing my frustration with our slow progress. I directed the helmsmen to raise and lower sails and fiddle with their trim to optimize our speed. Alfie commented on the lack of birds, fish, other boats, and pollution, saying that there was nothing in our world but *Dolphin*, the water, and the sky. The airless nights brought no relief from the oppressive heat, and Alfie had the good idea of moving his mattress to the cabin roof. It wasn't much cooler, but he appreciated the short commute when it was time to turn out for his night watch!

On March 17, the wind picked up to Force 2-3 and we were making a decent four knots under sail. The heat was still stifling, and Bob decided that he wanted to try a dip. I lowered him over with a double-knotted bowline around his chest, but the effort was not a success. It was pretty funny to watch Bob drag and spin helplessly in our wake, getting a thorough but uncomfortable wash. He groused around the boat for the next couple of hours until I had to speak to him about improving his attitude. Next I had a little discussion with Alfie about his hygiene and eating habits. I suggested he wash more frequently, drink a little more water, and eat fewer sweets. One scurvy crewman was enough! The hot tropical weather and my overall disappointment kept everyone on edge.

One morning I awoke to hear loud squawks and squeals. *Dolphin* had two uninvited hitch-hikers: a pair of grey and white mottled sea birds that balanced precariously on a railing for about five hours before flying away. Most days, we took a cooling dip in mid-afternoon, but one afternoon, some sea creature stung me right on my penis, leaving an itchy red welt about two inches long. I worried about what Réanne would think! The next afternoon I went for a quick swim. I felt something brush my leg, and quickly climbed up the ladder. I looked down to see turds floating by. Bob had flushed the head to get even with me for towing him behind *Dolphin* at four knots a few days before.

Relaxing on a sunny afternoon

On March 21, we toasted the vernal equinox with South African red wine. At 6°S, we were close to the equator, and the sun set straight down into the west. Venus lit the dawn sky, looking as bright as a ship approaching from the east. Jupiter shone as our evening star, setting about two hours after the sun. Ursa Major reappeared again in the north, and swells from the northeast caused *Dolphin* to roll as she felt the first influence of currents from the Northern Hemisphere.

Dolphin glided along under clear skies while the breeze rose and fell erratically through long hot days and nights that otherwise passed almost without incident. On a cruising sailboat, something always needs repair or adjustment, so constant upkeep was just part of our routine. Alfie spent one afternoon sewing a big rip in the mizzen staysail. I praised his meticulous stitches—they were better than the original sailmaker's work. Bob spent two hours refolding the stowed mainsail for better visibility forward, which was a hard job due to his weak legs. Margie continued to be a thrifty housewife in the galley. She served the last of the South African eggs. After thirty days without refrigeration, they were a little strong, but still edible. She also found three fruitcakes that Réanne had stowed in the bilges, but it was a disappointment to find that they were old and ruined. We spotted a huge oil tanker, the *Texaco Norway,* heading south and passing us within a half-mile. I reemphasized how important it was for the helmsman to scan the entire horizon every five minutes, and not let the Captain be the first to spot another ship. I also reviewed the abandon ship procedures and boat rules.

On March 22, our day's run was only ninety-three miles. Counter to the pilot chart predictions, we saw little wind and almost no current. The fuel gauge showed three-quarters full, and we'd run the engine for forty-four hours since St. Helena. Trinidad was still 2,500 miles away. I was discouraged by our lack of progress since I did not want to be late meeting Réanne. I radioed the Brazilian island of Fernando de Noronha and was told I could buy a drum of diesel fuel and 8 quarts of engine oil, so I decided to call in there. It wasn't far off our planned course, and the replenished fuel would keep us on schedule.

The wind remained fitful, sometimes reaching Force 2 with no change in the barometer. A large pod of dolphins accompanied us through the evening of March 23. Sheet lightning flashed low around the horizon. By noon the next day, we had pouring rain, and everyone gathered buckets for washing and laundry. It was wonderful to have a renewed supply of fresh water.

By evening we could see clouds along the horizon, lit from underneath with skyglow. Isla Fernando de Noronha was close! We dropped anchor at noon on March 25.

*   *   *   *   *

Ferdinand de Noronha is a volcanic archipelago, 220 miles from the coast of Brazil. The main island hosts a Brazilian army base and is distinguished by a phallic peak about 1,000 feet high called Morro do Pico. Discovered by the Portuguese in the early 1500's, the islands have been used as a supply stop ever since. Charles Darwin visited the main island during the voyage of the *Beagle*. Part of the *Beagle's* mission was to calibrate and rectify South American coastal charts, and the island served as one of the fundamental survey points.

During the time of our visit, the islands were under Brazilian army command, and we were not permitted ashore. This didn't bother me since I didn't intend to stay long enough for sight-seeing. I arranged for the diesel and oil to be brought out to *Dolphin*. We had enough time for me to give the hull a quick inspection and I was pleased to find it in fairly good condition. The only other yacht in the bay was *Calypso*, a Cheoy Lee 47 that had just finished a race from Durban, South Africa, to Rio de Janeiro, Brazil. I swam across and had glass of sherry with her captain, Alan Richards, while we discussed the fastest crossing routes. Later I was able to transmit a radio message to his family in Pretoria, South Africa. Alan eventually wrote a steamy book about his experiences sailing a small boat across the South Pacific with an all-girl crew.

We left Fernando de Naronha at first light the next morning, on March 24. I estimated that our passage to Trinidad would take about two more weeks. The crew was clearly ready for some time on land, and the sulking and bickering continued to increase. Large cross seas added to the tension aboard, but fair winds carried *Dolphin* along. Other ships became more common, and we often spotted two or three per day. On March 26, the DR position log showed us eleven miles off the Ilha de las Rocas, a volcanic atoll only 150 miles from the mainland of Brazil. In other words, we had re-crossed the Atlantic and were back in South American waters.

The weather became increasingly squally, with Force 1-2 winds succeeded by heavy gusts and rain showers. We had a little fun with the rain showers. When the helmsman saw squalls in the distance, he would alter our heading to take advantage of the rain. We each chose a place to stand on the deck and used a cup of fresh water each to lather up with soap and then rinse off with the rainwater. Everyone usually managed to have a decent shower, although once or twice I got all soaped up and the rain stopped before I could rinse off. I also spoke with Réanne. A fresh water shower and hearing her cheerful voice were the simple joys of life on board!

The humidity dropped and the breeze cooled slightly. In spite of this, I felt a little under the weather, maybe because Margie, Trev and I had drunk a liter of Smuggler's rum over the previous two evenings to celebrate our return to South America, the coup in Argentina, and talking with Réanne. On Saturday, March 27, we had more heavy rain. The weather grew muggier, with low visibility. Alfie dropped the stern running lamp overboard, and we had no replacement since I had already lost one in the South Pacific. This was a worry since ships were now regularly passing us within a mile or two.

That afternoon, we came alongside a Brazilian fishing boat. It was an open long-boat with a small place amidships for a cooking fire. The boat hardly looked sea-worthy, with flimsy rigging of home-made cloth sails, bamboo spars, and just an old anchor and some coral rocks for ballast. The seven men aboard were a wild looking crew, wearing ragged shorts and T-shirts. We assumed they were Brazilian. Although Alfie could understand some Portuguese, he couldn't understand these men. They must have been speaking some rough, rural dialect or an Indian language. When I first spotted them, I sent Margie below deck in case they made trouble about our beautiful, red-haired first mate.

Brazilian fishermen offshore

At that time, we were approximately one hundred miles off shore of the mouth of the Amazon River, where fresh water and debris mingle with the Atlantic Ocean. There was a strong offshore current and the men on the boat had no compass, nor any kind of navigational equipment. They presumably relied on knowing the currents and keeping the same bearing and angle to sail out to sea and back to their village. Using sign language and gestures, I traded several cans of fruit and clams for about eight kilos of fresh red snapper. The oldest of the men gave me a toothless grin and demanded my red swimming trunks as part of the trade. His companions had rather threatening expressions, so I passed my shorts across on a boat hook to the amusement of the old man. After this distraction in the middle of nowhere, we sailed on.

The weather continued changeable, and the depth varied surprisingly. Several times we saw uncharted shoals with depths of only eight or ten fathoms. The seas were rough, and we frequently observed other ships. The question became: "Why do ships at night always look like they are headed straight at us?" Rain squalls hit suddenly, once soaking everything in the cabin through the open hatches. After that we kept the hatches closed, which was suffocating with an air temperature of 85 °F. Nothing dried, and the cabin stank of mildew. Although conditions on board were uncomfortable, *Dolphin* was making good progress with daily runs averaging 130 miles.

Margie took an evening watch to give the helmsman a break. I chatted with her in the cockpit for several hours. I told her how much I missed Réanne, and she gave me another woman's perspective on Réanne's reasons for abandoning me and our voyage. She cited Réanne's teaching career in California, her less adventurous nature, and her expectations about marriage and family obligations. Margie also missed Réanne, and she told me that she found it tough to be the only woman in a group of macho males who did a lot of posturing and crude bragging.

Bob's health had not improved. The sores on his arms appeared to be infected, and he had red lines running up his arm, indicating blood poisoning. He felt feverish and really looked ill. Margie started him on a course of penicillin, and I told him he had to see a doctor again as soon as we arrived at Trinidad.

Margie making the most of the tropical sun.

The currents and shoals in this area off the coast of French Guiana and Suriname were tricky. We skirted various small islets and outcrops, keeping well away from shore for fear of uncharted rocks. The seas were choppy and unpleasant. Heavy showers pelted us while the winds picked up, but their direction was changeable, forcing the helmsmen to adjust sail trim and course constantly. I hadn't obtained a good sextant fix in two days, and the DR plot looked like a snake. The heat, humidity, and rough sailing added to the aggravation. Bob commented that we must be moving north since the weather was just like Chicago's. We'd eaten all the fresh food, and the crew continued to be in a quarrelsome mood, wrangling over imagined slights. Margie was cooking one afternoon when a huge lurch caused an upset in the galley. Dinner spilled all over the floor, making a big mess, and a broken jar sent shards of glass everywhere. I cut my foot on one of the slivers. Returning to business life in Los Angeles began to have some appeal.

By March 30, the squalls and rain seemed interminable. Everything was wet and mildewed. In the middle of an afternoon squall, Alfie hollered, "Fish! Fish!" and pulled in a nice dorado on Bob's homemade lure. My navigational plots showed that we'd crossed the equator. We motored on amid chop and squalls and celebrated our formal arrival in the Northern Hemisphere with fresh fish, a strawberry jam cake made by Alfie, and shots of brandy in apple juice.

*   *   *   *   *

The weather improved over the next few days, and we enjoyed smooth motor sailing followed by excellent progress under full sail. Seven dorado swam with us for an hour, appearing as gleaming streaks of blue and yellow. Sunshine made my noon navigation shot easy, enabling me to confirm our location, and bringing Margie up on deck in her bikini to work on her tan. I finished reading Graham Greene's *The Honorary Consul*—an excellent read and very true to life. Greene vividly described aspects of Argentine society that I had observed during my stay. The temperature cooled to 85 °F, and the humidity dropped. Polaris was visible low in the northern sky. It seemed like an old friend to me, although Margie and Trev were sorry to see the Southern Cross disappear below the southern horizon. The clear dark ultramarine of the equatorial current met the opaque green outflow of the Amazon in a tidal rip extending from one horizon to the other. Vertical waves smacked two or three feet in the air along the intersection. Once we crossed the current line, our speed increased by at least a knot. Always ready to celebrate, Trev and I toasted the Amazon with cocktails of gin and pomelo, and then enjoyed a siesta in the afternoon sun. The day's run on April 3 was 175 miles. I calculated that if we could maintain that rate, *Dolphin* would reach Trinidad within four days, a prospect that cheered everyone. Trev and I finished off the gin—we'd drunk a liter in two days, along with some wine. I put business cards into the empty bottles and dropped them overboard.

That night, Bob started leaping around and screaming like he had the DTs. I wrestled him to the floor and Alfie and Trev lifted him back up and tied him into his bunk, but he kept screaming until he collapsed from exhaustion. He seemed to be pursued by monsters. This was bad enough, but the screaming prevented me from listening for unexpected noises, like the sounds of lines rubbing and fraying. I resolved that as soon as we reached Trinidad, I would put Bob ashore and leave him there since his psychological and physical problems were more than I could handle.

Réanne and I had a long and discouraging radio conversation about the business and its ever-expanding problems. She told me things were deteriorating rapidly in my absence. I needed to be there in person to make some serious decisions about the company's future, and explain them to the Board of Directors. Facing up to my responsibilities, I decided that rather than meeting Réanne in Trinidad, I would make a quick trip back to California to deal with my obligations. Réanne cancelled her flight, and booked me round-trip tickets between Port of Spain and Los Angeles.

Dolphin was traveling once again in the main shipping lanes and we had to be extra vigilant. Her engine ran so loudly, that the helmsman had difficulty distinguishing the sound of engines from other nearby ships over the noise of our own diesel. I decided there should be two pairs of eyes in the cockpit at night. Bob, Margie, and I took turns sitting with the helmsman during the night watches

By 0030 hours April 7, we were within sight of land. The wind had died, and we motored past numerous small fishing dories and buoys lit up with kerosene lamps. We were enjoying the beautiful spectacle of the lights reflecting across the dark water when suddenly an unlit launch roared up to us at full throttle. The man aboard screamed at us unintelligibly. Eventually we understood that we were motoring right through his fishing nets, and I asked how best to escape them. The man followed us, still cursing vigorously, but he told me to steer straight ahead, which is what I would have done anyway. I apologized, and I certainly hadn't sailed over his set on purpose. It was an unpleasant welcome.

We arrived in Trinidad on the morning of our thirty-first day at sea since St. Helena and motored slowly into King's Wharf, San Fernando, the island's industrial capital. I radioed the immigration authority about Bob: "Uncontrollable situation, I can't deal with this guy." They directed me to anchor away from the dock, and Bob was subdued while I rowed him ashore with his suitcase. The Trinidadian authorities were apparently experienced in handling unruly crew and met us at the dock with an ambulance.

"I never had a family like you guys," Bob cried as we reached the dock. "This was the best time of my life!"

That was the last I saw of Bob, although Margie and Trev ran into him about a week later. He was staying at a backpacker hostel, and they reported that he seemed happy and upbeat.

I cleared Customs with no problem, and we continued into Port of Spain, anchoring near the Trinidad and Tobago Yacht Club. We all washed in fresh water without worrying about conserving it. Margie washed her long red hair. Her fantastically feminine appearance disguised the toughness of the woman underneath. Alfie shaved and swept his hair back with gel. Trev and I combed our beards and hair. We had all changed into clean shorts and our red team T-shirts with *Le Dauphin Amical* screen-printed in white. We were a motley crew, and ready for some shore leave.

Fish drying from *Dolphin*'s lifelines.

Chapter 11

Port of Spain, Trinidad to Balboa, Panama

7 April - 9 May, 1976

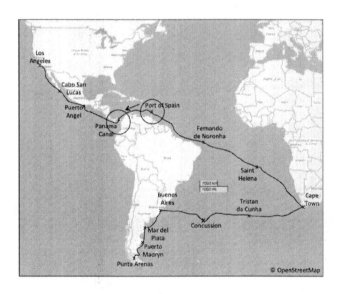

The islands comprising the nation of Trinidad and Tobago are generally considered to be the southernmost islands in the Caribbean, although geographically they are part of South America. Trinidad, the larger and more populous of the two islands, lies about seven miles from Venezuela's northeastern coast. Christopher Columbus came across the islands in 1498 on his third voyage, and Spain, France, and Great Britain all governed them at different times. All three colonial powers ruthlessly exploited the local inhabitants, whether native islanders, slaves from Africa, or indentured workers imported from other countries. This exploitation continued well into the twentieth century, leading to ongoing stresses among the various populations and classes of people. Trinidad has experienced several petroleum booms, and at the time of our visit it was quite prosperous and economically stable with a great deal of multi-national investment, perhaps fueling social friction. The islands are the birthplace of calypso music and the steel drum, said to be the only acoustic musical instrument invented in the 20th century.

Trinidad left me with a negative impression. Garbage and debris choked the poorly paved streets. Peeling paint and slip-shod repairs characterized the grimy buildings and there were cockroaches everywhere. There was also obvious hostility directed toward white folks. When we checked in with Customs and Immigration authorities on our arrival, my white crew and I were told to wait until all of the black customers had been served. In the streets, we were repeatedly and aggressively forced off the sidewalk and into the road by black people. This was my first experience of racial animosity directed at me personally, and I found it quite disturbing. It was quite a contrast to my experiences in South Africa as an unwilling member of a privileged minority.

The people of Trinidad and Tobago had been given administrative independence from the British government in 1962. During the time of our visit they were in the process of abolishing their links to the British monarchy. Great struggles over black power and unionization were being waged both in the government and in the general society, perhaps explaining some of the hostility we experienced.

Port of Spain was to be *Dolphin*'s home for the next three weeks while I flew back to California to deal with the escalating crisis at WGI. Before I left, I paid for a guest berth at the Trinidad-Tobago yacht club, and we tied up to our assigned mooring buoy. Once cleaned up, we all went to the yacht club dining room and ordered sandwiches. The setting was wonderful as the dining room and bar floated on a covered barge. There were no sidewalls, and we could see *Dolphin* bobbing gently at her nearby mooring. Overhead, large brass fans kept enough of a breeze circulating to repel the vicious tropical mosquitoes, and the dim lighting and cooler air were extremely relaxing. The friendly Jamaican bartender, Jemit, introduced us all to the local rum punch, concocted of tropical fruit juices and a local white rum. It was a real "punch" too, since it could knock your socks off! Jemit was tall and black, and he developed an immediate crush on Margie. His impressive skills with the cocktail shaker entertained us as he threw it high in the air and caught it behind his back with a flourish and a beautiful smile.

During my absence, Margie and Trev socialized with some of the expatriate residents, visited mansions and exclusive beaches, and danced to calypso and steel drum music. I returned from California under a lot of pressure from my Board of Directors to return home immediately and take active control of the business. I needed to get *Dolphin* across the Caribbean, through the Panama Canal, and up the coast of Mexico as quickly as possible. As we prepared to leave, several different people requested that I carry a "package or two" for them to friends in the States, but sensibly, I declined. Other people warned me to watch out for drug runners at sea. They generally drove fast boats with no running lights, but they carried sophisticated radar which I hoped meant they could easily spot and avoid us. We motored away in minimal wind and balmy heat on Saturday night, May 1. In the middle of the night, Trev heard a high-powered engine running on our starboard side, but he couldn't see any lights on the other craft, and it quickly passed by. We had several similar near-encounters on our trip across the Caribbean.

Though we had left Bob behind in Trinidad, *Dolphin* still had five people aboard. A friend of Margie's from South Africa, Liz Borrowman, had been visiting Margie and Trev while I was away. Liz was a lovely blonde Scottish lass about Margie's age. I invited her to be my guest for the four-day passage to the island of Curaçao, and she agreed to join us.

The wind picked up to Force 3-4 in the early hours of the morning and we enjoyed good sailing again. Six to ten foot swells rolled us along. Liz felt queasy and rested below. The rest of us quickly regained our sea legs and enjoyed the vigorous conditions. We sailed through the dark waves under starry skies, with the sound of a dolphin blowing air beside the boat. The lapping water, the strumming halyards, and the creaking rigging were wonderfully soothing after the grimy weeks ashore. I found it challenging not to hoist too much sail and overstrain the cracked main mast. Alfie did not understand my caution, and several times he put up more sail than was safe. Liz eventually felt better and joined us on deck. She took a turn steering the boat and began to enjoy the rollicking ride. A shade cloth over the helm kept the sun from burning us during the daylight hours.

Margie, Don, and Liz between Trinidad and Curaçao.

We made good progress for several days in Force 3-4-5 winds and six to ten foot seas. These swells were the largest we'd encountered since leaving the Strait of Magellan. Sometimes they combined into waves whose heights reached twenty feet. The dolphin-striker under the bowsprit frequently tapped the water, and the bow wave sometimes spread twenty feet out in front of us. I was vigilant in enforcing everyone's use of safety harnesses on deck, since the disorganized waves kept the boat pitching wildly. We also had to be careful to keep the cabin closed since water occasionally swept over the deck and ran into any open port or hatch. On one occasion, it even put out the stove. Trev remarked that no self-respecting cockroach would be seen aboard in these conditions. Margie replied that unless the cockroaches had gills, they'd all drown!

*   *   *   *   *

By the evening of May 3, we were off the island of Bonaire twenty-five miles from Curaçao. Bonaire is the easternmost of the three Caribbean islands off the northwest coast of Venezuela, known from their initials as the ABC group: Aruba, Bonaire and Curaçao. The three islands have a complicated political history as outposts of varying status within the now mostly defunct Dutch empire. The Spanish mariners who first discovered the islands in 1499 dismissed them as "useless," other than as a source of slave labor for the copper mines on Hispaniola Island (now Haiti and the Dominican Republic). From our vantage point at sea as we sailed past, Bonaire indeed appeared quite dry and barren.

A few hours later, we saw the lights of Curaçao on the horizon, and by 0600 hours we were tied up at the Harbor Master's dock in Willemstad, the capital. Passport control in Willemstad was very efficient. The immigration officers enjoyed reading the Afrikaans written on Margie and Trev's South African passports, since Curaçao had been under Dutch control since the seventeenth century, and Dutch and Flemish were widely spoken. After clearing Customs, we all took short naps. We all awoke to a wonderful aroma as Liz fried bacon and eggs and brewed fresh coffee. Alfie carried in croissants he bought at a nearby bakery. He told us that he had just followed his nose to find them.

We tied *Dolphin* up along a waterfront canal lined with attractive, multi-colored Dutch and Spanish colonial style buildings. I found Willemstad picturesque and attractive. The first-world cleanliness and order impressed me after the squalor of Trinidad. In Punda, the oldest part of Willemstad, sidewalk cafés were packed with chattering tourists and locals alike, all enjoying pastries and drinking coffee or beer. Spanish, Flemish, Dutch, Portuguese, and English conversations filled the air in this cheerful blended community. An open-air market sold fruit and vegetables, spices, sunhats, and souvenirs.

Willemstad was (and still is) a popular stop for the Caribbean cruise ship industry. Two large cruise ships were in port that day bringing streams of eager sightseers. The tourists bartered for souvenirs while the locals bought groceries and were greeted with familiar nods from the vendors. Trev, Alfie, and I bought fresh provisions and arranged for fuel and water. Margie and Liz bought keepsakes, had their hair cut, and Liz booked a flight back to Trinidad for that afternoon. We all met up at a Punda café and sat outside at a table with a bright red umbrella. We savored our lunch of fresh salad and local beer as well as the stable ground since we knew it was only temporary. After saying goodbye to Liz, we said our own farewells to Willemstad. Shortly afterward, the pontoon bridge swung open to release us from our canal berth, and *Dolphin* set sail for Panama.

*   *   *   *   *

The passage to Panama took six days, from May 5 until May 11, 1976. The wind blew at Force 4-5 for the first day, with clear skies. *Dolphin* bowled along, covering 146 miles in the first twenty-four hours. The swells averaged ten feet as the wind began to rise and howl in the rigging. Seawater flooded the cabin when a big wave poured down the open hatch. The wind and waves continued to increase, and the mechanical log began to pop clear of the water at times. We were an experienced crew by now, and generally enjoyed the bouncy conditions. Pop music blared from the cassette player during the afternoon, but cooking was out of the question as the seas grew ever larger. We made do with fresh tomatoes, bananas, and avocados, as well as crackers, cheese, and bread. Trev and I enjoyed another rum punch the first evening.

By the third day, the wind had reached Force 7. As *Dolphin* tossed over twenty-five foot swells, the fuel cans stowed under the dinghy worked loose and began to slide around. Alfie clawed his way forward and lashed the cans back into place, wedging them with tires and a life jacket. *Dolphin* was laid on her beam-ends among the huge swells. The starboard jib tore under the strain and waves broke over the stern, pooping the helmsman several times. Chunks of foam broke from the waves and blew in streaks between the swells—Force 8! These were easily the roughest conditions we'd experienced since leaving the Strait of Magellan. In spite of this, we ran 210 miles in forty-

six hours, and by midnight, we had only 165 miles to go to reach
Panama. Conditions eased, and we were able to raise more sail
and quit fighting the ocean.

By Saturday, May 8, my navigation plots and the
increasing amount of vessel traffic around us confirmed that we
were nearing the port of Cristóbal, at the Atlantic entrance to the
Panama Canal. The wind dropped to almost nothing, but the seas
continued to be choppy and confused. *Dolphin* rode awkwardly
and the sails flapped unpleasantly as we motored on. Around
1400 hours on Sunday afternoon, May 9, we sighted the
breakwater enclosing Bahía Limón and the port of Cristóbal. I
radioed to announce our arrival, and was given instructions on
where to anchor. *Dolphin* was required to fly the yellow
quarantine jack until a Customs officer came aboard and we
filled out the necessary arrival documents. Then I went to shore
to spend several hours obtaining the documents for our transit of
the Panama Canal. The crew was left marooned on the boat for
the rest of the afternoon, although they enjoyed a good meal and
a rest after the rough passage from Curaçao.

Our Canal transit was scheduled for Tuesday, May 11.
This would require us to spend a day and two nights in port, as
paying guests of the Panama Yacht Club, a private establishment
catering to both local boat owners and visiting cruisers. Given
the choice of tying up to a dock or a mooring buoy, I opted to tie
to one of the mooring buoys since it was less expensive than
tying to the dock and seemed safer from intruders. It also
allowed us to use the club's services, including the showers and

laundry facilities, a bar, a restaurant, and a grocery store. We all took advantage of the showers, then walked downtown to a sidewalk café. Everyone always seemed to crave red meat once we were in port, and we enjoyed sizzling filet steaks wrapped in bacon with salad and Argentine red wine. The next day, while the crew topped up fuel, water, and bought fresh groceries, I spent several hours visiting a series of officials in the Port Captain's office, filling out yet more transit paperwork.

Of course, there were fees associated with every aspect of the transit process. I paid cash at the bank, then showed the receipt to all the various offices so we could be scheduled for the actual transit. The basic fee was calculated by vessel length, and the supplemental fees were the same for all ship sizes. The complete transit cost about U.S. $250, including all the supplemental fees and charges. That was in 1976 dollars. In today's dollars, the cost for an average private sailboat is around $1,000 - $3,000, and the average toll for ships is around $50,000.

The Panama Canal was constructed with commercial ships in mind, but provision was made for the numerous small vessels and pleasure craft, *Dolphin* among them, that cross the isthmus. Vessels like ours had to meet certain criteria in order to be allowed to make the passage. This included the ability to maintain a speed of at least five knots; otherwise we would be denied transit, or have to be towed or barged through the Canal at greater expense. *Dolphin*'s trusty Cummins diesel was in good working order and capable of maintaining the required speed, so we were cleared for the transit.

As a small vessel, *Dolphin* had to share the locks with other, larger vessels, and since she was a sailboat with protruding masts and spars, she would transit the locks "center-chambered"—that is, as far from each of the side walls as possible, to prevent entanglement and damage to the hull and rigging. Because of strong turbulence as water rushed in and out of the locks, we needed to have six 100-foot lines tethering the boat to the shore, and six sturdy people on deck to handle the lines in order to keep the boat in position. We were able to hire two people from the yacht club to help us. Terry and Sharon frequently worked as line-handlers, assisting pleasure boats like *Dolphin* to transit the Canal, and they told some interesting stories about life in the Canal Zone as we chatted during our long day together.

We were also required to take aboard a transit advisor who would direct *Dolphin*'s operations through the canal, and who maintained radio contact with the lock operators, other vessels, and so forth. Our advisor was Pilot Captain Richard Heer. We were required to provide him with "proper meals" and drinks while he was aboard, an awning to keep the sun off while he was in the cockpit, and suitable WC facilities. Pilot Captain Heer was a regular Captain Bligh. He was quite pompous, yelling instructions to those of us on deck and shouting elaborate food orders down to Margie in the galley. He even demanded ice for his drink, which was a laugh since *Dolphin* had no facility for ice making. At one point, we were alongside a large cruising boat from Los Angeles, the *Alicia Dawn*. I asked if they could spare some ice, but the skipper was quite unfriendly and hollered back "No," without even a "Sorry." Margie resented being bossed around by the Pilot Captain and shouted at him, "Don't talk to me like that. You don't order me around! You'll get what I'm making." We agreed afterwards that a Canal Pilot's job appeared to be pretty comfortable, and that it probably took good connections within the Canal Zone to get it.

The Panama Canal is forty-eight miles long. The entire passage, from the Atlantic port of Cristóbal to the Pacific port of Balboa, typically takes fourteen to sixteen hours, with a transit time in the actual Canal itself of eight hours. In our case, we left the Panama Yacht Club in Cristóbal with Pilot Captain Heer and our line handlers at 0700 hours, and we tied up at the Balboa Yacht Club and discharged them all at 2200.

Dolphin started her traverse in Limón Bay which narrowed into a two-mile long channel forming the approach to the Gatún Locks. The sea level section of the Canal on the Atlantic side is six and a half miles long. It runs through a mangrove swamp only a few feet above sea level in most places so it isn't particularly scenic. Things became more exciting as we approached the first of the three Gatún Locks, and Pilot Captain Heer gave the go-ahead to proceed. The three locks took ninety minutes to raise us eighty-five feet, bringing us to the level of Gatún Lake, the huge fresh water lake that comprises the middle of the passage. All of the lock chambers are of the same rectangular dimensions—110 feet wide and 1,000 feet long with wide steel gates that closed solidly behind us. The gates are seven feet thick and covered with riveted plates, like the hull of the *Titanic*, reaching as high as eighty-two feet above the water level.

We were positioned sideways in the lock chamber behind a much larger vessel, a westbound cargo ship that was apparently unloaded. It rode high enough in the water that its huge propellers were visible, and only ten feet away from us! *Dolphin* was tethered to the top of the lock chamber by heavy lines that came down from large bollards or cleats and passed through *Dolphin*'s deck cleats. The six line-handlers stood evenly spaced all the way around the boat, poised to shorten the lines in order to maintain tension as *Dolphin* rose in the chamber. The looming propellers of our companion ship were motionless, but there was plenty of excitement as the lock began to fill. A three-foot high wall of murky water charged at us out of conduits in the sidewalls as the control valves opened. The wave was full of debris and seaweed, and the rushing water echoing around the chamber was so loud that it was hard to hear the orders of the Pilot Captain. The line-handlers worked furiously to keep tension on the lines, but *Dolphin* still bounced around like a cork as we rose about thirty feet in five minutes.

Over the next hour we repeated this nerve-wracking process twice more as we negotiated the second and third Gatún Locks. Combined, the three locks stretch over a distance of about a mile and a quarter; a similar series of locks lowers boats in and out of Miraflores Lake at the Pacific end of the Canal. Each set of locks is paired with another set of locks located immediately alongside used by vessels traveling in the opposite direction. This pairing allows water to be pumped from one set of locks to the other, raising ships on one side, while the other side is lowered, thus conserving some of the vast amount of water required to operate the canal.

It was a relief to motor out of the third Gatún Lock and into the peaceful expanse of Gatún Lake. This large lake covers much of the interior of the Isthmus of Panama. We saw a few buildings on shore, and there were several large ships anchored in the lake waiting for their turns in the locks. *Dolphin* stayed right on schedule, motoring through the lake along a shipping channel marked with numerous buoys. The crew passed the time eating lunch and looking for alligators in the lush rainforest that covered the lakeshore and numerous islands. The relentless sun beat down, and we all perspired heavily in the intense heat and humidity.

After winding our way through the lake for twenty-four miles, we reached the small town of Gamboa and the beginning of the Gaillard Cut. (The name was changed from Gaillard to the Culebra Cut after Panama took control of the Canal zone from the U.S. in 1999.) Gamboa, originally built to service the workers who dug the Cut, is now home to the Panama Canal Dredging Division and a handful of other mid-Canal employees. The village had a pleasant, sleepy ambience, but we had no reason to stop and motored on into the Gaillard Cut. Apart from the locks, this is the most "canal-like" part of the Panama Canal. The cut is an almost straight, nine-mile-long stretch of water running from north-northwest to south-southeast, with sloping sides rising to 300 feet on either side. More than 25,000 laborers perished during construction of this section of the canal, many of them from landslides, during the removal of more than 230 million cubic yards of rock.

Eventually we reached the first of the three Pedro Miguel Locks at the Pacific end of the Canal and began our descent to Balboa. The procedure here was the same as in the Gatún Locks, but in reverse. Lowering the water required the line handlers to pay out the restraining lines while maintaining a steady and even tension as the boat dropped within the lock chamber, so that *Dolphin* would remain in her central position. However, one of the crew misunderstood my instructions and tied off the line to the deck cleat. Suddenly there was a huge *craaaack* and the steel cleat ripped right out of the deck, line and all! On the plus side, the turbulence from the water draining from the lock wasn't as strong as in the ascending locks, so we weren't in real danger. Still, I was pretty upset about the damage.

The Pedro Miguel Locks are not quite a mile long. They discharge into Miraflores Lake, a small man-made body of water that connects to the two mile-long Miraflores Locks. In turn, these locks empty their contents into the final short section of channel that opens into Balboa Harbor and the Pacific Ocean. We negotiated this last set of locks without incident and proceeded to the nearby Balboa Yacht Club. At this point we discharged Captain Heer and our two line handlers, dumped the old tires we had bought in Cristóbal to use as fenders in the locks, and bashed the stern against a piling. Poor *Dolphin* suffered another wound, but at least she and I were back in the Pacific and ready to start the final leg of the voyage and the sprint toward home.

Chapter 12

Balboa, Panama to Long Beach, California

9 May - 25 June, 1976

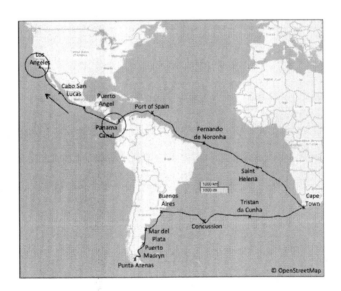

We did not linger in Balboa, but sailed out into the Pacific that same night, and with a moderate wind, set sail for California under an almost full moon. *Dolphin* rounded the peninsula of La Cacao, at the tip of Costa Rica, with the mainsail up and the engine moving us steadily on. We steered well away from the rocks and sandbanks of Isla Cebaco off to our port side.

Since we were sailing in the shipping lanes again, we had to be vigilant. A coastal steamer passed within 200 yards, and the slapping of its large wake against our wooden hull woke me. We rolled so strongly that the center hatch and dinghy oars almost fell overboard, but fortunately the oars had been tied down. The sea was irregular and confused, the light wind we'd started with had dropped, and *Dolphin* fought a strong adverse current. After a second close call with a passing tanker, we reverted to double duty for the night watches, with the helmsman steering and either Margie or me watching for other vessels.

Soon after daylight, Alfie spotted a dark object floating in front of us and called for me to take a look. It turned out to be a hand-carved mahogany dugout canoe about half full of water and with a few resident crabs. It was about fifteen feet long and extremely heavy, but I decided we should bring it aboard, a task that took two hours. Margie thought this effort was a waste of time, but I was intrigued with the canoe as a cultural artifact and displayed it at my home in California for many years.

The echo sounder read sixty fathoms plus, so we were well out on the continental shelf with lots of water beneath us and no reefs or shoals. Our main danger was the constant vessel traffic. On the second evening, a huge container ship bore right down on us. I monitored the angle of its lights as it approached and confirmed that the vessel was on a direct collision course with us. I illuminated our mainsail with the spotlight and computed that we had four minutes in which to be noticed. Otherwise, we would have to untie all of *Dolphin*'s preventers and make an abrupt change of course. After my second flash of the high beam spotlight, the container ship turned about fifteen degrees to port, saving us the work of coming about.

We welcomed another pod of dolphin companions. These beauties were a mottled black and white, with white lips and noses. I imagined they were smiling in celebration of my second birthday at sea, on May 13. Our own *Dolphin* continued sailing off shore, passing along the coasts of Nicaragua, El Salvador, and Guatemala. We were out of sight of land but could see the skyglow from the cities and we enjoyed the musky smell of tropical vegetation well out to sea.

When we went swimming, Margie and I discovered that the Pacific Ocean was warmer than the Atlantic. We sighted many more sharks in these waters than we had in the Atlantic, as well as a few lone sea turtles. Trev and Alfie kept watch for sharks, and we didn't stay in the water long, perhaps ten minutes each day. It was refreshing and made a good change of perspective. The slight risk of encountering sharks added zest to our daily routine, while Alfie continued to marvel at our foolhardiness.

Over the next few days the weather varied wildly, from steamy tropical sun to thunder and lightning storms with plenty of rain squalls so we could shower. The hazy visibility and humidity were balanced by beautiful blood-red sunrises and sunsets. The waves continued choppy, and the engine began to run roughly. I suspected contaminated fuel, either from buying dirty fuel in Panama or from stirred-up sediment in the tank.

Alfie and Trev spent a grimy, sweaty day draining the tank and filtering the fuel. Their efforts seemed to help the engine run a little smoother.

By May 23, we were in Mexican waters and headed for the mainland to stock up on supplies. Lightning, thunder, and squalls blasted the boat in the pre-dawn darkness, while three dolphins escorted us to shore. Their phosphorescent splashing and lively play entertained us delightfully for several hours. A Force 2 breeze drove us toward the small fishing village of Puerto Angel, a day's sail away. We raised the genoa along with the mainsail to maximize our speed. The shade cloth over the cockpit protected us from the noonday sun, and we enjoyed a lunch of fresh fried dorado, accompanied by three-bean salad and a second mixed salad of pine nuts, cherry tomatoes, arugula, and mozzarella cheese, topped with balsamic vinegar. Life was sweet!

Land finally came into view at 2000 hours. We approached cautiously in the last of the twilight. Tiny lights twinkling along the coast greeted us, and we dropped anchor in forty feet of water some 300 yards from shore. The next morning, we took the dinghy into Puerto Angel. This was our first port of call in Mexico, but no officials came out to greet us, and no one ashore asked to see our passports. Puerto Angel was a picturesque village with single-storied buildings painted in colorful hues and draped in tropical foliage. More important to me, it also had a bank, a gas station, several small general stores, two restaurants, and an open market selling fresh produce and meat. We bought tacos for lunch from a street vendor, relishing the fresh spices as a change from shipboard fare. Margie and Trev enjoyed haggling with the vendors and were pleased when they got a peso or two knocked off the prices of items they wanted. I bought a few gallons of diesel fuel but decided to refuel *Dolphin* more fully in the larger town of Puerto Escondido further along the coast. I reasoned that fuel bought in a larger town would be less expensive and less likely to be contaminated. I could buy enough fuel there for *Dolphin* to motor all the way to Cabo San Lucas if necessary.

Puerto Angel's sleepy pace appealed to all of us. It had not yet become the over-developed tourist town it is today. After our tacos, we sat on the beach sipping cold drinks and enjoying the sun and a swim. Later, we rowed the dingy back to *Dolphin* and spent the last of the afternoon reading and napping on deck. As the sun lowered to the horizon, we prepared for an evening back on shore, anticipating fresh food and a change of surroundings. The twilight cast a turquoise sheen across the water as we rowed the dinghy to the beach.

After choosing a restaurant, we ordered beers and our customary steak meal, this time with *champignons* and salad. Ice cold beers arrived and we chatted at our window table. Suddenly Trev lifted up his feet and shrieked like a little girl—the floor was a seething mass of cockroaches! "Urghhh!" Our meal arrived, but none of us could relax and enjoy it with the multitudes of gross insects scurrying around our feet. I kept my own feet up on the chair beside me. Trev wouldn't stop humming *La Cucaracha*. It was a relief to row the dinghy back to our roach-free home. Margie made sure we carefully shook out our clothing and sandals before we climbed back aboard *Dolphin*.

Early the next morning, we watched three men fishing from shore with throwing nets. Margie and Trev had often seen this technique used near Cape Town, where it was called "trek netting." The ten to twenty foot diameter nets were round or oval and weighted down at a few places around the edges. The men threw the nets out horizontally with a spinning motion so that they unfurled across a wide area of water. The weights quickly pulled the nets to the bottom, rewarding the fishermen with a haul of small wriggling fish. With shouts and arm waves, a lookout posted higher up the hill directed the fishermen toward schooling fish.

That afternoon, we resumed sailing up the Mexican coast, hugging the coastline and staying only about five miles from shore. Even from that distance we could see heavy surf crashing along the beach, manifesting the power and energy of the Pacific swells as they collided with land after thousands of miles of open sea.

A favorable current allowed *Dolphin* to make excellent speed and we anchored in Puerto Escondido's small bay in the hot sun of the next afternoon. An American named Andy swam out to us and offered to help me buy some diesel. Once ashore, he took me in his pickup to a small gas station up in the hills where I bought two drums of fuel. Trev and Alfie transferred the contents into *Dolphin*'s fuel tanks, and then we pulled up the anchor and headed back to sea.

Our next port of call would be Cabo San Lucas at the southern tip of the Baja Peninsula. Réanne told me via a ham radio patch that a couple of the Directors were maneuvering to gain control of the business by using my prolonged absence as an excuse. I needed to make another trip back to California to confront them. I set a direct course for Cabo, although this meant we were committed to sailing in the shipping lanes. Vessel traffic was extremely heavy, and we had multiple close encounters with large, fast-moving cargo ships, as well as with tugs towing barges with very limited maneuverability. We continued doubling up on the night watches for additional safety, but this meant that everyone was tired and increasingly irritable from insufficient sleep.

On May 28, we arrived in the broad expanse of Acapulco Bay. Even then, Acapulco was far too commercialized to entice us to stop, but we enjoyed the display of opulent homes and hotels draped across the cliffside in architectural splendor. With a light wind blowing and minimal sail, we cruised across the beautiful bay feeling like jet-set tourists.

I was back in familiar waters. Twenty months earlier, *Dolphin* had departed from Acapulco to Easter Island on the first leg of my intended circumnavigation. Retracing my steps was a painful acknowledgement of my collapsed ambition. Now I only wanted to finish the trip as quickly as possible.

From Acapulco, we headed north to a small and apparently uninhabited island called Isla Grande and dropped anchor for the night. Alfie and Margie cooked a meal of stir-fried canned turkey with mushrooms, green onions, broccoli and fresh pineapple, served on a bed of white rice. They seemed to become ever more creative with the menus as the days passed. That night we all sat out on deck enjoying the sunset and the warm weather.

The crew thought that I had gone crazy the next morning when I insisted that everyone swim ashore to Isla Grande. They could see only the deserted beach with a rocky backdrop. Alfie donned his *grande* shoes and a life jacket, while Trev, Margie, and I wore our bathing suits. Margie looked as stunning as ever in her black bikini. The swim ashore was refreshing and we sat on the beach chatting and drying off in the sun. Then I suggested we take the opportunity to stretch our legs one last time before swimming back to *Dolphin* and setting sail.

The crew followed me up a sandy bank to the highest point of the island. At the top, they got the surprise of their lives! On the northwest side of Isla Grande was another beautiful sandy beach ornamented with a *palapa*, or palm-thatched hut, and a couple of cocktail tables shaded by thatched umbrellas. A few boats were moored in the bay and about a dozen people were on the beach, sipping tropical drinks and eating pizza while Mexican music blared from a speaker. We ambled down to sit on the wooden benches and chat with the other sailors. I already knew about the resort on Isla Grande from a previous visit and had brought my wallet wrapped in plastic and secured in the pocket of my trunks. I bought a round of piña coladas and we shared a huge pizza with cheese and salami. It was a good morale-booster too, since our voyage was drawing to a close. I wanted to show my appreciation for my crew's hard work and loyalty.

Back aboard *Dolphin*, we all slept for a few hours before setting sail again late that night. I estimated we were 240 miles from Cabo San Lucas. I planned to fly to Los Angeles from Cabo for twelve days. The crew looked forward to more Mexican hospitality in my absence.

A steady southeast wind kept us sailing directly toward our destination. We could have called into Puerto Vallarta, since the resort town's beautiful golden beaches beckoned, but my business couldn't wait. A day or two later, as we crossed the Gulf of California, the engine started acting up. Rather than dirty fuel, the problem this time was the transmission. I couldn't get the engine into gear at all. I made a radio contact with Réanne, and she found a mechanic in Cabo who could take a look at the engine while I was away. Of course, I was completely confident that *Dolphin* could sail the remaining sixty miles to Cabo without an engine. The Force 2 winds were favorable, and we moved steadily along—apart from a ten-minute break so Margie and I could take a cooling dip. Trev kept his usual lookout for predators. Just as we climbed back into the cockpit, a five-foot long shark came over to inspect us. Yikes—we could have been a meal for that toothy guy!

We ate an early dinner on deck as the sun set over the calm sea. I have always loved the turquoise twilights in this part of the world, and the tranquil setting gave me a chance to reflect on the approaching end of my dream. Regret for the collapse of my plans and longing for Réanne mingled with my desire to roll up my sleeves and run my company properly again.

We sighted the headlands of Cabo San Lucas on June 4 and dropped anchor that afternoon about 50 yards from the main beach. Customs officials came out and cleared us for official entry. I didn't mention that we'd already landed on Mexican soil on Isla Grande and Puertos Angel and Escondido.

I spent the next twelve days in California trying to resolve a succession of corporate crises. Margie sent a letter to inform me about the boat repairs and how she, Trev, and Alfie were spending their time.

Life here is sweet. [she wrote] *We are spending the days casually: sleeping late, cooking breakfast, lazing on the beach, eating lunch in a* cantina, *and shopping at the local market for fresh food. Since you left, the sea has stayed calm with light breezes, but we have found a more protected anchorage east of the point if a storm blows up and we need to move* Dolphin *to more secure waters.*

About five days ago, with no advance warning at all, a guy named Doc motored up to us. He said he was the mechanic, so we invited him aboard, and he took a bunch of the engine apart. Then he said he needed some parts, and he left without telling us when he'd be back or how to get in touch with him, so I was kind of anxious about it. He came back a couple of days later, completely serviced the engine, and fixed the transmission linkage. Trev thought the work was excellent and paid him the $200 you left for repairs, while I thought the relaxed way he came and went really illustrated the mañana *spirit!*

When I returned, I was pleasantly surprised at how eager the crew was to head back out to sea. The day after my return, we refueled and filled the water tanks at the Cabo San Lucas cannery and headed to California. Once we'd left Cabo, Margie told me of the alarming incident she and Trev had experienced in my absence.

A couple of nights before you got back, Trev and I wanted a treat, so we went to the Hotel Cabo San Lucas on the main street. It's kind of swanky and expensive, but we just went for a margarita and antipasto. I wore my new maxi-dress, with my bikini under it, in case I got wet rowing the dinghy. Some visiting Mexican farmers chatted us up in pretty good English. They were curious about us, since they could tell we were obviously foreign, but we weren't sunburned like most tourists. They bought us something I'd never tried before: a round of drinks, shots of tequila with salt and lime on the side. It was pretty good!

The three men were sugar farmers on a golf vacation. They kept asking us to join them for dinner, so we finally did. We were all having a good time telling stories, joking, and drinking, until I noticed that Trev suddenly seemed extremely drunk. He was almost incapacitated! I thanked the three men, and managed to get Trev wobbling out toward our dinghy on the beach. I had to half-carry him and half-drag him, and the three big guys weren't any help—they came along with us, but they were just laughing and shouting and carrying on. When I got to the dinghy, one of the oars was missing! I shoved the dinghy out into the water and tumbled Trev into it, where he promptly passed out.

One of the men followed me out to the dinghy, and he picked me right up into his arms! He carried me back to the beach and set me down on the sand. They were all very drunk and now they were only speaking Spanish. One of the other men tried to lift me up and kiss me, and I could see the dinghy start to drift away out to sea! Two of the men managed to get my dress off, revealing my bikini. I realized I was in serious trouble, alone on a dark beach with three big, drunk men. I stood up, shoved the closest man away, ran full force into the shallow water, and dove hard toward the dinghy. It was already about forty feet away, and I swam for my life! I got to the dinghy, and pulled myself in. The men on shore shouted obscenities.

Alfie called from Dolphin, "Are you okay, Margarita?"

"No, I only have one oar and I'm just going around in circles," I yelled back.

"Swim back here", he hollered.

I was seriously tempted to leave Trev and the dinghy and do just that! I tried not to think too much about the large sharks that I'd seen lately, dove in, and pulled the dinghy along by the painter back to Dolphin. It took about 15 minutes. Alfie was there to pull me up and secure the dingy. I was very shaken. He got me a blanket and made a mug of hot chocolate. We couldn't figure out how to lift Trev onto the boat, so we decided to cover him with a blanket and leave him there to sleep it off. Let the seagulls poop on him!

Clearly, land sharks could be more dangerous than sea sharks!

*　　　　*　　　　*　　　　*　　　　*

After Doc's repairs, the engine ran far more smoothly than before, and we made good time with a light southerly wind. I wanted to make progress while we could since sailboats traveling up the west coast of Baja California are frequently impeded by strong winds blowing from the north. The coastline studded with palm trees along the long golden beaches cried out for a visit, but I delayed a beach stop for a couple of days. The water temperature was a tempting 75 ºF, but the presence of numerous huge sharks deterred us from swimming off the boat.

In honor of our own Margarita, we took a final shore break on Isla Margarita, on June 18. We had crossed the Tropic of Cancer, meaning that *Dolphin* was north of the sun at its zenith for the first time in eighteen months. We trimmed the sails and motored carefully through a narrow passage between two points, navigating to a small beach on Punta Cayuco. Sea lions basked on the rocks along the approach to the beach. Their hoarse calls echoed from the rocks, and Alfie in particular enjoyed watching them, although we could smell them from all the way across the bay.

We dropped anchor opposite an isolated cove of ochre-colored sand. It was a picture-postcard sea front, where low hills dotted with wildflowers formed the backdrop. Absolutely transparent turquoise water lapped onto the beach, and we passed a perfect three hours diving overboard, swimming, going ashore, lying on the beach, and soaking up the sunshine. The wind picked up and I called, "Time to get going to California, guys!" Reluctantly, we headed out to sea. The Force 2-3 breezes were pleasant, but the voyage was fast coming to an end. Contradictory feelings continued to trouble me—nostalgia for the good times and wild adventures we had shared, and frustration with the unsatisfying ending to my dream of circumnavigation.

Alfie mending yet another rip in *Dolphin*'s worn sails

The next morning brought the first Pacific fog. This phenomenon arises when the cold North Pacific waters, which circulate this far south, are struck by hot breezes from the desert interior. The fog isolated us in our own little world, distorting any sounds and making progress imperceptible. Alfie busied himself repairing another tear in the mainsail. His neat, tight stitches were so impeccable that I would have trusted him to suture a flesh wound. Not for the first time, I reflected that *Dolphin*'s crew possessed a great range of skills.

*   *   *   *   *

As the fog lifted, we saw a few seals bobbing about. Further on, two feisty dolphins competed for "king of the bow." The amount of birdlife increased and I spotted a pelican, another sign that we were getting close to home. In the distance, a flock of Man-o-War frigate birds hovered in place over a school of fish. These magnificent birds have long black wings that span at least six feet. One or two had brilliant scarlet breasts. Hoping to catch a fish or two ourselves, we changed tack to meet them and set a trawling line, but had no luck.

The weather cooled as we progressed north, and the fog became a daily morning visitor. The decreased visibility made the depth sounder my most important navigational tool as I kept *Dolphin* motoring along the six fathom contour. Proceeding mostly under engine power, we continued our schedule of four hours on watch and four hours of sleep, and two people were on watch for other shipping at all times.

On June 24, I calculated that we had crossed the Mexico-U.S. border. The fog thickened as we neared San Diego harbor, creating the illusion that *Dolphin* was suspended in mid-air. Trev stood lookout at the bow, only forty feet from the cockpit, but I couldn't see him. Other boats surrounded us. The fog distorted the sounds, so we couldn't tell where they were coming from. We could hear people aboard fishing boats and other vessels clanging pot lids together, ringing ship's bells, and blowing horns. Voices called "Hello? Hello?" from all directions. For over eighteen hours, we stayed alert, reading the echo sounder and straining to see anything through the fog.

My chart for the San Diego harbor entrance showed the Navy submarine base to our port side. I hugged the right side of the channel but couldn't make out the dangerous pilings that should have delineated the margin. We searched for the red entrance buoy, but cold, hunger, and lack of sleep were making us all edgy and confused.

Looming out of the fog, a large tanker overtook us close to starboard. It blew its whistle right behind us, giving me huge jolt of adrenaline. The ship's radar had enabled them to avoid colliding with us. The adrenaline fueled a flash of brilliance, and I decided to increase engine speed and follow closely in the wake of the huge vessel, drafting it like a racing bicyclist. That kept us safe as we tucked in right behind her. Standing at the bow, Trev could barely make out the bulk of the ship's stern looming high above us. He watched for any variations in the ship's speed or course and shouted his reports back to me while Margie read depths off the echo sounder. I couldn't see anything but the huge wake on either side of us. As we entered the harbor, the fog lifted slightly, and I saw the Customs dock to our right. We peeled off from our mother ship and rang our bell in thanks for the escort. The tanker replied with two loud toots—truly a friend in deed.

U.S. Customs officers boarded *Dolphin* and we proceeded to fill out the necessary paperwork. Margie had to surrender our last Mexican potato, dashing hopes of fries for dinner with the last of the yellowtail tuna. The officers also refused entry to our two twelve ounce bottles of Bacardi rum, but I wouldn't let them confiscate it. I put four yellow plastic mugs on the table and we drank the contents of both bottles mixed with a little orange cordial and fruit juice. I reasoned that since we had all been awake for more than eighteen hours, it was technically our cocktail hour. We accomplished this impressive feat in just over two hours. The officials refused to let us sail inebriated, and ordered us to remain at the Customs dock for at least the next six hours.

Inebriated or not, we cooked the yellowtail for dinner and ate it with bread that Alfie had baked the day before. We were ravenous and it was delicious! The Customs officers found us pretty amusing and gave us a lot of latitude. Maybe they thought we deserved a little celebration after our long voyage.

On Saturday, June 25, after a good nine hours sleep, we departed San Diego for the final leg of *Dolphin's* journey. A fair wind of Force 2 sent us northward through familiar waters, past Dana Point, Newport Beach, and Sunset Beach. At 1300 hours, we entered the port of Long Beach. I shocked my crew by motoring *Dolphin* straight up to the big drawbridge. The warning sirens sounded and the bells rang, stopping the heavy traffic. The span opened like a triumphal archway. We motored proudly through into Wilmington where we tied up at Fellows Marina.

Stained, patched, and mended from more than 20,000 hard miles, *Dolphin* was a sight to behold. A few people greeted us with waves as we passed by, but I was grateful that we had no welcoming committee—not even Réanne knew the exact time of our arrival. *Dolphin* had returned from a 622 day voyage that was the partial fulfillment and ultimate thwarting of my life's desire. I was in no mood to be gracious to people who could have no comprehension of what *Dolphin* had been through and no understanding of the gifts she'd given us—the awe-inspiring sights, the companionship born in sharing hard work and danger, and the exhilaration of living life to its fullest. To onlookers, we were merely a motley crew on a worn and tattered boat, but *Dolphin—Le Dauphin Amical*—was a boat that had been well and truly sailed.

Appendix 1

Le Dauphin Amical Specifications

Documented number: 524917
William Garden Porpoise Class Ketch
> 42 ft. on deck (not including bowsprit and dinghy davits)
> 13 ft. beam, 5/4 ft. draft
> 20 tons gross, 19 tons net hull
> Strip-planked Port Orford cedar over oak ribs
> Full-length composite cement and iron keel
> Hull built in Victoria, B.C., Canada
> Finished in Port Angeles, Washington (1969)

Rigging:
> Spruce masts
> Stainless steel standing rigging
> Dacron running rigging (six sail halyards, three signal halyards)
> Booms with downhaul, outhauls, topping lifts and preventers with block and tackle
> Permanent boom gallows (main and mizzen)

Winches:
> Four halyard winches mounted on masts
> Two each two-speed Barlow sheet winches

Vane:
> Self-steering custom-built auxiliary trim tab (wind-operated)

Lifelines:
> Double stainless steel, plastic-covered lifelines
> Full bow and stern pulpits, stainless
> Port and starboard lifeline harnesses on deck, stainless

Accommodations:
> Sleeps six
> Double bunk amidships to starboard
> Single pilot berth to port
> Double quarterberth bunk aft
> Galley settee converts to single berth
> Single pipe berth in forepeak
> Berths have either bunkboards or weather clothes

Engine:

Perkins 4-107 diesel (with factory spares)
Five batteries charged from two alternators
Three separate fuel filters 100+ gallon iron fuel tank

Sails:

Dacron main
Yankee working jib forestaysail (self-tending)
Genoa
Twin spinnaker jibs with forespar running poles
mounted to mast
Mizzen staysail (cotton, antique)

Galley:

Shipmate two-burner with oven (kerosene)
Sink, deep double-compartment, stainless steel
Fresh and saltwater manual pumps
Water capacity: three stainless tanks, 120 gallons, plus plastic
jerry jugs backup
Gimballed table, solid teak, with L-shaped settee to starboard

Cabin sole: Armstrong vinyl with stainless steel trim

Head:

Wilcox Crittenden mounted fore and aft
Sink and cupboards

Forepeak:

Workbench to port with vise and tool rack
Single pipe berth mounted to starboard
Three chain lockers

Ground Tackle:

65 lb. Danforth
60 lb. CQR
50 lb. fisherman
50 lb. yachtsman
20 lb. Danforth
Anchor winch: Simpson Lawrence, two-speed
Rodes: 300 ft. BBB 3/8 in. chain
300 ft. 7/8 in. nylon
300 ft. 5/8 in. nylon
Various spare lines, chain, and shackles

Heater:

Shipmate fireplace (coal- or wood-burning)
Stainless steel full reflector and chimney

Navigation:

Seafarer echo sounder
Salem quartz crystal chronometer 6 in.
Danforth Constellation compass 2 in.
Tell Tale compass

V.D.O. knotmeter and sumlog
Walker taffrail log
Single sideband transceiver for ham bands
300 charts of world ports,
Plath sextant, stopwatch, hand-bearing compass, misc.
Survival Gear:
Eight-man Avon life raft
Special abandon-ship locker with equipment
Three fire extinguishers
Eight life jackets
Two life rings with xenon lights
Two man-overboard poles
Miscellaneous:
Two large full-length deck sun shades
Fourteen opening portlights (most with mesh screens)
Lazaret aft of wheel steering
Three hatches for ventilation (including main companionway)
Bosun's box of spare parts
Variety of jerry jugs for water, diesel, and kerosene
Two spotlights
Two boat hooks
Two Whale gusher bilge pumps (one mounted on deck)

Appendix 2

Celestial Navigation

The sextant is an instrument used to determine the position of a boat at sea from the known position of an object in the sky such as the sun, moon or stars. A sophisticated version of the standard school protractor, it relies on the measurement of angles and trigonometric calculations, rather than electricity or satellites, and has been the standard navigational tool for sailors and terrestrial explorers for almost 300 years. It is still relied upon as a back-up navigational aid for ships even in these days of satellite navigation. A sextant can also be used to measure distances to objects of known height—a mountain peak or a tall lighthouse.

The sextant gets its name from the "protractor" (or measuring) part of the instrument. This is a curved sector that is approximately one-sixth of a circle (60°), marked with a graduated scale. Other basic components include a moveable arm, a sighting telescope, and two mirrors. The index mirror is mounted at the top of the moveable arm and the horizon mirror is in a fixed position on the frame of the sextant. When the operator looks through the sighting scope, he or she can see images simultaneously in each mirror, side by side. The operator positions the sextant so that the fixed mirror produces an image of the horizon. He or she then positions the moveable arm until the bottom edge of the sun (or moon or star) as it appears in the index mirror lines up with the horizon as it appears in the fixed horizon mirror. A filter on the index mirror prevents eye damage from looking at the sun. The position of the arm relative to the graduated scale on the sector can then be read off to give the angle of altitude.

This might sound simple (or not) in theory, but it's difficult to get an accurate angle in practice, particularly on a rocking boat. I would take six to ten sightings at one minute intervals around the time of "local" noon each day (i.e., when the sun approached its zenith). I would end up with a series of angles, and then use the highest one to calculate our position.

Latitude is computed by taking the angle (altitude) of the sun in the sky at its noontime zenith, and converting this measure, via published nautical tables, to a north-south position relative to the equator and the pole of whichever hemisphere you happen to be in. It can also be calculated from the position of certain stars, such as Polaris, the Pole Star. Ancient mariners, from the Greeks onwards, used basic forms of sextants to measure solar, lunar and celestial positions relative to the horizon, then converted the resulting angles using trigonometric formulae into latitudinal positions on Earth. Degrees of latitude translate to fixed north-south distances: a difference of one degree, for example, as measured by sextant from one day to the next, equates to 69 miles (111.2 kilometers) sailed.

I also used the daily sun shot data to figure out our longitude, by noting the time on our shipboard chronometer at which "local" noon occurred. Longitude is the boat's east-west position relative to the Prime Meridian, an imaginary line between the poles which passes through the Royal Observatory in Greenwich, England (deemed by historical convention to be Longitude 0°). If your shipboard chronometer is set to the time in Greenwich, longitude can be calculated from the difference between 1200 hours Greenwich Mean Time (GMT) and the time of shipboard "local" noon. This is because the Earth rotates every 24 hours at a uniform rate around the axis between the north and south poles. One hour of difference between local noon at sea and noon in Greenwich equates to 15° of planetary rotation, which provides the longitudinal position relative to the Prime (0°) Meridian. This measure translates to distances sailed depending on latitude, however. One degree of longitude at the equator is 68 miles; at the poles, it's zero miles.

To avoid having to do numerous sun shots to find out when local noon occurs each day, I would look up an estimate beforehand from time and longitude tables published in a book for mariners called *The Captain's Nautical Almanac*. I also had a pretty good idea from one day to the next, just from doing the daily sun shots. As we sailed east across the Atlantic, local noon was a few minutes earlier each day. On the later westbound leg, local noon got progressively later.

Though the radios aboard *Dolphin* were out of action after our pitchpole in the southeast Pacific, for all of our Atlantic voyages, from Punta Arenas onwards, I was able to use time signals broadcast over shortwave radio to check the accuracy of our chronometer, and thus of my daily longitudinal estimates.

Old-time mariners had a harder time of it, and before the development of an accurate nautical chronometer in the 18th century, by British clockmaker John Harrison and others, longitude could be determined (with difficulty) only from sextant sightings of certain stars, and relating their measured positions to those in published tables. Captain Cook was one of the first navigators to voyage with one of the new chronometers, and to test its accuracy against that of the heavens.

Appendix 3

Beaufort Wind Scale

Sir Francis Beaufort (1774—1857) developed the wind scale, which also describes sea and land conditions accompanying the wind force.

Beaufort Number	Descriptive Term	Mean wind speed equivalent in knots	Mean Wave Height m/ft	Sea Conditions
0	Calm	> 1	0	Flat
1	Light air	1 - 3	0-0.2 m 0-1 ft	Ripples without foam crests.
2	Light breeze	3 - 6.4	0.2-0.5 m 0-1 ft	Small wavelets; crests have a glassy appearance and do not break.
3	Gentle breeze	6.4 - 10.6	0.5-1 m 2-3.5 ft	Large wavelets; crests begin to break; scattered whitecaps.
4	Moderate breeze	10.6 - 15.5	1-2 m 3.5-6 ft	Small waves with breaking crests, frequent whitecaps.
5	Fresh breeze	15.5 - 21	2-3 m 6-9 ft	Moderate waves of some length. Many whitecaps. Small amounts of spray.
6	Strong breeze	21 - 27	3-4 m 9-13 ft	Long waves begin to form. White foam crests are very frequent. Some airborne spray is

				present.
7	Near gale	27 - 33	4-5.5 ft 13-19 ft	Sea heaps up and white foam from breaking waves begins to be blown in streaks along the direction of the wind.
8	Gale	33 - 40	5.5-7 m 18-25 ft	Moderately high waves with breaking crests forming spindrift. Well-marked streaks of foam are blown along wind direction. Considerable airborne spray.
9	Strong gale	40 - 48	7-10 m 23-32 ft	High waves; dense foam blown along the direction of the wind; crests of waves begin to roll over; spray may reduce visibility.
10	Storm	48 - 55	9-12 m 29-41 ft	Very high waves with long overhanging crests; the resulting foam, in great patches, is blown in dense white streaks along the direction of the wind; on the whole, the surface of the sea takes a white appearance; the tumbling of the sea becomes heavy and shock-like; visibility affected.

11	Violent Storm	55 - 63	11.5-16 m 37-52 ft	Exceptionally high waves (small and medium-sized ships might be for a time lost to view behind the waves); the sea is completely covered with long white patches of foam lying along the direction of the wind; everywhere the edges of the wave crests are blown into froth; visibility affected.
12	Hurricane	63 and over	> 14 m > 46 ft	The air is filled with foam and spray; sea completely white with driving spray; visibility very seriously affected.

Glossary

aft: toward the rear or stern of the boat

anchor rode: anchor system that includes anchor and chain or line

angostura: narrows

backwind a sail: to push the sail out to one side to catch the wind on its back side until the boat turns the opposite way

backstay: a stay that runs from the masthead to the stern

bahía: bay

bare poles (to barepole): to sail downwind without any sails in very strong winds where the spars and hull provide adequate surface to propel the boat

beam ends: sides of the boat. The name derives from the cross timbers of the boat.

bend a sail: install a sail

bobstay: a lower steel support that offsets pressure on the jib stay (mounted below bowsprit)

boom: horizontal spar

boom gallows: a frame that holds the boom stationary after the sail is lowered

bow: front end of the boat

bowsprit: fixed spar projecting from the bow

broach: a sudden, uncontrolled turning of a boat broadside to the wind or seas; usually results in a capsize

bulkhead: a transverse wall of a boat

cable: 600 feet

caleta: cove

capsize: rolling over of the boat by wind or waves

catheads: timber "arms" to which the bowsprit stays are secured

come about: to turn from one tack to the other, with the bow passing through the eye of the wind

companionway: entranceway (also see: hatch)

darsena: basin or inlet

deckhead: the ceiling of the interior cabin

doghouse: that part of the cabin which sits above deck (also known as deckhouse)

dolphin striker: a nearly vertical rod which helps tension the bobstay

douse the sails: to take down the sails

draw: when a sail fills with wind

drogue: a sea anchor or object towed off the stern of a vessel to keep the vessel end-on to a heavy sea

eye of the wind: the direction the wind is coming from

fall off: to turn away from the eye of the wind, turn downwind

feather into the wind: adjust the sails to lessen the effort they exert on the boat

fetch: the distance waves travel in open water before they reach a certain point; the longer the fetch, the higher the waves

fordo: fjord

forepeak: the forward most part of the sailboat

forestay: a stay that runs from high on the mast to the foredeck

forward: toward the front or bow of the boat

frames: the ribs of a boat

galley: the kitchen

gimbals: pivoting rings that hold a stove, compass, or table to allow it to tip or rotate so that it remains level as the boat moves around it

gybe: to change direction so that the wind comes from the opposite quarter and the stern moves across the eye of the wind; this maneuver can be dangerous to the boat and crew, unless it is carefully controlled

halyard: a line used to hoist a sail, or other things, aloft

hatch: an opening in the deck

head: toilet

headstay: steel stay which runs from the bow (or bowsprit) to the top of the foremast; usually supports the jib sails

heave to: to remove sail or engine power so as to remain nearly stationary in the water

helm: the wheel or tiller of a boat

irons, in: loss of headway

isla: island

lazaret: storage compartment in the stern of a boat

let out: to pay out a line in the direction of the tension

lie ahull: a "last-ditch" maneuver used when weather conditions are so severe that the boat or crew can't cope with continuing to sail and stand watch; the boat looks after itself under bare poles and assumes its own position with regard to the wind and the waves; usually handled by lashing the helm, closing all hatches, and going below *lifelines:* lines run through the stanchions along the sides of a deck to prevent crew from falling overboard; also, a safety line run along the length of deck which a crew member can hook into

luff: the leading edge of a sail; to luff: to come into the wind, causing the sails to wave back and forth.

mizzen mast: the aft mast on a ketch-rigged sailboat

mechanical log/patent log: a trailing spinner connected to a revolving counter mounted on the transom of a boat which indicates how far in nautical miles a boat has travelled

paso: passage or pass

pitch: the fore and aft plunging and rising of a boat

pitchpole: when a boat is tossed end over end by waves

point into the wind: to sail toward the direction of the wind

port: the left side of a boat looking toward the bow

portlight: porthole

preventer: a strap or line that ties a boom in position when the boat is sailing downwind, so that if the angle of the wind shifts there is no unintentional gybe

puerto: port, harbor

rail: the edge of the deck, usually raised

roll: the sideways motion of a boat

salon: the main living area

Samson post: a heavy post and bitt on the foredeck used to fasten the anchor line

sheets: lines that control the lateral movement of a sail

shrouds: stays that run from either side of the mast to the deck

sole: cabin floor

spars: the general term for masts, booms, etc.

spreaders: horizontal struts used to tension the shrouds

stanchions: metal posts used to hold the lifelines along the deck

starboard: the right side of a boat looking toward the bow

staysail: a small sail attached to the forward side of the mast, aft of the jib

step: where the base (heel) of a mast is set

stern: aft or rear of boat

strakes: lines of planking

tack: change the boat's direction by adjusting the sails so the wind is coming from the other side

warp: a heavy line used in towing a drogue

williwaw: wind of high velocity that sweeps down the sides of a mountain

yaw: to swing horizontally off course, as when a boat is running with a quartering sea

50328578R00158

Made in the USA
Charleston, SC
22 December 2015